Releasing Our Dragons

Letting go of addictive
and compulsive behaviours

~ a lived experience ~

Mac,
  I hope this book brings insight + inspiration in your own life journey.
          Dianne

DIANNE SZYMANSKI KRYNICKI

◆ FriesenPress

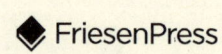

One Printers Way
Altona, MB R0G 0B0
Canada

www.friesenpress.com

Copyright © 2021 by Dianne Szymanski Krynicki
First Edition — 2021

All rights reserved.

No part of this publication may be reproduced in any form, or by any means, electronic or mechanical, including photocopying, recording, or any information browsing, storage, or retrieval system, without permission in writing from FriesenPress.

ISBN
978-1-03-911513-2 (Hardcover)
978-1-03-911512-5 (Paperback)
978-1-03-911514-9 (eBook)

1. SELF-HELP, SUBSTANCE ABUSE & ADDICTIONS

Distributed to the trade by The Ingram Book Company

This is the book I wish I'd had in early recovery. It is like a dear friend guiding you through your journey, pointing out pitfalls and reminding you of your strengths. Even for those further on in their journey of recovery it is a comfort and an inspiration. The courageous depths of the honesty found in these pages are a roadmap for the reader to find their own depths of courage which they may not have known they possess.

– Crysta Fernandez

This inspiring book is a must-read for anyone who has suffered adversity or attempted to change behaviour only to fall back into the old pattern. With honesty and courage, Dianne engages us in her journey of healing to overcome the dragons that cause inner conflict in her life.

– Diane Frederick, RN, MA, ICADC, ICCS (ret)

As a recovering alcoholic for thirty-four years, and a meditator for seven years, I have read numerous books on both subjects, but this is a book everyone in recovery should read. I appreciate Dianne's courage in sharing her journey through counselling, Alcoholics Anonymous and meditation. This book is bang on, and brilliantly presented. An excellent read for anyone suffering at any level or type of addiction.

– Patricia Pielow

Dianne's book is straightforward and to the point, yet is written from the heart. There is a lot of reason to be hopeful about the prospect of recovery with serenity. Her examples and stories will give you the information you need. The rest is a matter of time and work.

– Shinzen Young, Co-Director of SEMA Lab,
Author of *The Science of Enlightenment*

For
Kody and Willow,
with so much love and gratitude

Table of Contents

	A Lived Experience	1
	Reflection Exercise	4
1.	If Not Now, Then When?	9
2.	Why Do I Need to be Cool?	17
3.	Mindfulness	23
4.	The Art of Living	31
5.	The Gift of the Gobsmack	37
	Sacred Path Card #44 - Sacred Space	43
6.	I'm a Bad Person	45
7.	The More-is-Better Switch	53
8.	The Pull to Hibernate	59
9.	Highs / Lows	65
10.	Our Scars Mean We Have Survived	71
	Sacred Path Card #13 - Coral	77
11.	Letting Go	79
12.	Compassion and Loving Kindness	85
13.	The Grieving	93
14.	Don't Give Away Your Power	101
15.	Gratitude	109
	Sacred Path Card #40 - Great Smoking Mirror	115
16.	The Drama Dragon	117
17.	Pain is Our Teacher	123
18.	You Are Not a Victim	129
19.	Retain / Replace / DEPRIVE	135
20.	Relapse	141

Sacred Path Card #25 - Pow – Wow	145
21. Start Again	147
22. Being a Role Model	151
23. Accountability	157
24. Find Your Sangha	163
25. Be Your Own Mrs. Dubose	169
Sacred Path Card #19 - Painted Face	175
26. Learning to Have Fun	177
27. It is in Giving	183
28. 2020	189
29. A Taste of Freedom	195
30. Defining Moments	201
Creator Said	207
Epilogue	209
Resources	213
Acknowledgements	215
Works Cited	217

A Lived Experience

Do you consider yourself an addict?

I'm willing to bet that posing that question may have triggered an urge to close this book and put it down with an emphatic "That's not me!" resounding through your mind.

Me too.

And most people who know me would scoff at the idea.

"YOU?! C'mon, you're over-exaggerating the situation!"

We all have preconceived images that come to mind with the word addict, and more than likely your own image is not part of that. And it's worth noting that the dialogue is evolving regarding substance abusers; 'addict' has now been replaced with 'person who has lived experience.'

What is your lived experience? Obviously, there's a reason why you picked up this book.

Google says an addict is: "A person who is addicted (never use the word in its definition!) to a particular substance, typically an illegal drug."

Does that rule out alcohol, because then you're an 'alcoholic'? But you are still addicted (again, use of the word) to a particular substance.

Oxford Dictionary states: "An enthusiastic devotee of a specified thing or activity." Ha! I have always been the MOST enthusiastic, MOST devoted—in substance use—of all my friends and acquaintances.

The Cambridge English Dictionary defines an addict as: "A person who cannot stop doing or using something, especially something harmful." But I've 'stopped' many times. Problem is, I start again, and when I start, I don't stop.

And there's this detailed description found in a variety of addiction treatment websites: "Addiction is a primary, chronic disease of brain reward, motivation, memory and related circuitry" (what??). Wait, there's more: "Dysfunction in these circuits leads to characteristic biological, psychological, social and spiritual manifestations. This is reflected in an individual pathologically pursuing reward and/or relief by substance use and other behaviours."

Okay, there's a whole lot going on there. First of all, in the reference to 'circuitry,' it's our internal wiring being referenced, and yes, the more we repeat behaviours, the more reinforced and oh-so-familiar they become. And a pathological pursuit is a kind euphemism for an obsessive, compulsive, chronic, irrational, unreasonable pursuit, preoccupation, fixation... it's an unending list of negation, deprecation and destruction—of the self.

This one speaks to me. This addresses my ongoing pattern, and the psychological stranglehold I've experienced to varying degrees for much of my life.

Welcome to my lived experience.

This has been my lifelong battle, and continues to be my battleground. The cycle of excess, repetitive behaviours, remorse, and self-deprecation is a well-worn path that has become rutted into my psyche. And though I've had a successful career, been a responsible citizen and somehow managed to raise two amazing and well-balanced beings, it has continued to reside within, sometimes changing shape, sometimes pretending to be resolved, but always lurking, waiting, biding the time till—again and again—I reach for its deceptive comfort.

Perhaps you have also struggled with behaviours that don't sit well with you, that recur again and again despite your well-meaning intentions otherwise.

Perhaps you struggle with those two or three glasses of wine—or two or three bottles of wine—that inevitably end your day.

Or the fact that you can't seem to get through a day without marijuana, or cocaine, or whatever your drug of choice.

Or the hundreds or thousands of dollars you can't stop yourself from spending on stuff you really don't need even when you know your family will struggle to get to the next paycheck.

Or your craving to eat compulsively to the point of obesity, or the anguish of bulimia.

The list is endless and as varied as we are as individuals. And yet the preoccupation and obsession and pathological pursuit are the behaviours we share.

Despite tenets to the contrary, we are not each completely 'unique'; we share more similarities than differences and have much to learn in our connections. It is my hope and intention that this book speaks to others who feel trapped in adverse compulsive behaviours—to you—and that my lived experience can serve to shed some light as you forge your own way in your own journey.

Reflection Exercise

Congrats to you for reaching out for help in your journey. That first step is often the hardest—admitting to yourself that things are not good and you do not want to continue in the direction you've been going.

Many of us don't know how to start, and reaching out to those we know can be difficult because we may not be ready to admit our failings to them. That's okay. It's most important to realize it for yourself. After all, you're the one who is responsible for you, and you're the one who needs to be honest within yourself.

Baby steps.

Baby steps lead to steadier walking, and hiking, and climbing, and running and leaping for joy.

How to start?

Reading this book is a good opener, and doing your own inner work is the next step. You will most likely note that there is a lot of reference to facing your personal pain and discomfort in many of the entries. That's exactly what this is about: that is the road to recovery and change and inner peace. Our pain shows us our personal path.

After each chapter there is a reflection exercise to help guide you, with a reminder to settle yourself in a quiet space and become aware of your breath to help you to reach a calm state. These exercises are only suggestions that may be useful in prompting your work and getting you started. Use them in whatever way feels right for you. You may have a different approach that works for you, and that's even better—it is *your* work, *your* journey.

A Lived Experience

When doing your inner work, it is important to find a quiet space where you will not be interrupted for a period of time. That time frame is up to you and is dependent on your lifestyle, responsibilities, living arrangements and also the issue you are choosing to address at the time. You may need only twenty minutes, you may need a half day... and you may need a professional to guide you.

Choosing to confront our 'dragons' can be daunting. Please reach out to others if needed. You are choosing a very courageous path and seeking guidance in some form is recommended, may be helpful, and in some cases, is necessary.

I wish you calm, clarity, and perseverance. It may be a long road ahead, but it is oh, so worthwhile.

Do Not Let Sleeping Dragons Lie

*To find our answers we all must enter our own stillness
where our truths wait for us
under our Sleeping Dragons.
It is well known that dragons guard treasures.
Do not let them lie.
Because Sleeping Dragons LIE. They deceive. They make us believe
things about ourselves that are not true.
Wake them, prod them, kick them out of your being.
It's a scary undertaking, no question. There are mounds of stories to sift
through, fears to forge, sadness that corrodes our fortitude, angers to
release as they shake and rumble through our being.
It takes courage to keep moving, one foot after the other, through that
darkness, allowing its expression, releasing our Sleeping Dragons as they
roar their shame and guilt and fury. We watch them howl, allow them their
time on the stage, and trust that they will lose their force and slink away.
Let them roar, ride the rumbles, watch them wither.
Allow them their outrage. They are not us.
After each storm, we are still standing, not destroyed, but cleaner,
lighter, stronger.
And then. . .there it is. The Stillness. Our inherent treasure.
The stillness that gives us our peace, our happiness, our answers, our
truths, our pure Joy.
It is the noblest journey, step by challenging step, to Know Thyself.
Keep walking.*

– Dianne Szymanski Krynicki

one

What we are is a process that is continually unfolding into the unknown of each new moment.

— Joseph Goldstein,
Seeking the Heart of Wisdom

If Not Now, Then When?

My sixtieth year is tattooed on my soul.

It was the year when I could no longer ignore the Universe's intermittent tapping on my shoulder, and once I retired and then took a life-shifting ten-day Vipassana meditation course, that tapping became a consistent, persistent prodding, with a constant refrain of "If not now, then when?"

If not now, then when indeed. Life continues to present new situations to occupy our time: we date, we may couple or marry, we may choose to raise a family, and all the while we are absorbed with survival. We educate ourselves, find employment, earn enough money to provide shelter and sustenance in greater and lesser degrees, and try to dodge the chaos that is nearly always present or looming in some form as we develop our personal coping methods to make it through to the next day.

In my case, the compulsive coping pattern reared its ugly head very early in my life—the moment I was introduced to the sweet oblivion of alcohol. I got drunk for the first time at the age of twelve at a Polish wedding, throwing up outside behind the bushes at the Polish Legion Hall. Yup. Twelve years old. Gotta love those Eastern Europeans who see no harm in giving their buddy's daughter a drink, or two, or three. Of course, as kids we'd take turns going to the bar, so they wouldn't keep track. And it didn't take much for me to be intoxicated.

Then there's my sixteenth birthday celebrated at a seedy bar in the basement of a local restaurant, bragging to everyone after my fifth or eighth Singapore Sling (gross!) that I was only sixteen.

How about the time when, still underage, I woke up on the floor of a bathroom stall at another local bar around 4:00 am, to find that the bar had closed without any of the staff realizing I was still there, and my friends had all left thinking I'd gone home with someone else. I had no money except enough change to call a cab from a pay phone and luckily the driver agreed to come back to my home later for the fare. When my mother questioned me later about my whereabouts that night, I said, "You don't want to know." And neither did I. I did not want to acknowledge the depths of my degradation.

Those were the early days.

Fast forward through five decades of partying through high school, joining a cult, losing my licence due to an impaired driving charge, returning to school and educating myself for a career, becoming a parent, going through a separation, and navigating through all the stress and struggle with either a glass in my hand or a joint in my mouth.

Many of us have developed those behaviour patterns that are now detrimental because we needed them to help us cope and get through the day-to-day demands and struggles of difficult families or relationships or simply survival. And for many of us, the thought of making a change that means losing that comforting coping strategy is super scary. There is *always* a completely valid and worthwhile reason to put it off. Or we make our eighty-seventh attempt at a 'new day, new me' only to 'fail' once again.

So when is the 'right time'? Is there a 'right' time, a perfect moment to begin?

If you've ever attended an Alcoholics Anonymous meeting, you'll have heard the bottoming-out stories. Recovering alcoholics will remind themselves often of what their lives were like when they'd hit rock bottom, because they know they never want to be there again. And they know that that place could be only a drink away. . .because one drink is *never* enough. For some of them, that rock-bottom moment became their 'right' time to make a change. It was either that or an early grave.

Rock bottom looks different for everyone. In my mid-twenties I lost my driver's licence due to driving while impaired--*very* impaired. Losing my licence at that time meant losing my job, so it actually turned into a positive as I saw it as the perfect time to go back to school, something I'd been contemplating through my succession of unfulfilling employment positions. I took it as a slap across the head from the Universe—"No, go THIS way!"—and was grateful for the redirection.

But I didn't stop drinking. It wasn't until I became a parent and knew I could be jeopardizing my children's safety that it became the right time for me.

That was one 'right' time. I was to experience many more as I kept shifting my compulsive behaviours in order to maintain my coping and numbing strategies.

And the most insistent "If not now, then when?" was the writing of this book, because I could not write the book that was screaming for conception within me until I got—at least somewhat—to the other side, until I was willing to walk without reality-altering substances and see it through.

For decades I have used a cherished set of *Sacred Path Cards*, claiming "the discovery of self through Native teachings." At times of indecision or struggle or pain or doubt—or at any time—I would shuffle the deck and stop to pull the card when it felt right (as you continue reading, you will see that in between the sections of entries, I've included a few that have been very helpful and meaningful at various times in my life). This one in particular, #29, *Storyteller*, would show up time and time and time again:

> *The Storyteller card speaks of expansion on all levels. You are now growing and encompassing many new ideas if you have received this card. See which area of expansion needs your attention and feed your personal Fire of Creation. Create more and enjoy the expansion, knowing you earned it.*
>
> **Note that the expansion will continue if you are willing to share how you achieved your success with others. Many lives are influenced by another's story. In the good fortune of your present situation you may be instrumental in encouraging others.**
>
> *In all cases, expansion occurs when people are allowed to grow at their own rate and with their own understanding. The wisdom of the Storyteller is a part of the art of remembering. Note that you are now remembering your personal Medicine and how to* be *your potential.* (Sams 227 – 228)

The key words here are "how you achieved your success." Well, no wonder every attempt at starting a writing project fizzled out immediately. I could not write to help others without helping myself first, without achieving at least some modicum of success and understanding for and within myself.

And it was no coincidence that, for my retirement and sixtieth birthday, my daughters had enrolled me in one of Martha Beck's online writing courses, Write into Light. It was something I really wanted to do, but couldn't manage in my budget, so those two dears orchestrated it and recruited some other family members to donate to the cause, much to my delight and gratitude. After that, I felt even more pressure to make good on my lifelong intention to write and publish and prove their gift was not in vain, so I am forever grateful to them all.

Once I knew in my heart that the 'when' was 'now,' the writing flowed and gushed forth almost effortlessly, entry after entry, chapter upon chapter, and it was never an effort to sit myself down to write. I wanted to write it, I needed to write it; it had all been building within me for decades, and now was the time.

This book is my attempt to write the compulsive behaviour out of me.

Journaling has been my personal therapy for most of my adult life and I have successfully used my pen to manifest my thoughts on the page and positively manipulate them to create change. I've looked for books which speak to my situation, yet never found the right fit, so I decided to take the plunge and create one, knowing intuitively that it would help me as much as it could help others.

Your 'right' time does not need to be earth-shattering, life-altering or rock-bottoming. Every step, no matter how small, every slight shift you choose to make in filling those damning ruts in your psyche with something other than the compulsive habitual detrimental steps of the past makes a difference. And each one of these differences adds on to the other. At times our shift is barely noticeable, but the patterns in our wiring still get slightly shifted, and the next time they shift a little more, and within time they are rewiring themselves with each new way of thinking or each new reaction.

Don't beat yourself up for not following through with what you should do each and every time, and don't feel that 'all is lost.' At times all you can manage are baby steps, and at times you get off the path completely and just take a seat on the side and stay awhile. And yes, unfortunately sometimes you walk back to those places you really didn't want to visit ever again.

But each attempt means something and is worth something. Applaud yourself for each step, every 'new me' moment, every shift in your thinking. And accept and embrace those times when you're not strong enough, and know they will pass. Everything changes, and your perspective will also.

The right time is every time you make a different and better choice for yourself than you have in the past.

There are many, many, many more right times ahead for you.

The hope is that they never end, because they mean your journey keeps going, your life keeps changing, your true you keeps developing.

The right time is now, and the next now, and the next now.

Reflection

Position yourself comfortably in your quiet space. If writing appeals to you, have pen and paper ready, or better yet, a journal.

Close your eyes, and simply focus on your breath. Be aware of breathing in, breathing out, breathing in, breathing out, breathing in, breathing out.

The following questions or statements may be an aid to direct your inner work:

What is your rock-bottom moment? Do you have more than one? (Don't worry, most of us do).

If you have made it a practice to keep it buried deep down below your consciousness, gently, slowly, allow it to come to the surface, and revisit it, knowing that is not where you are at present. What brought you to that point at that time? Can you forgive yourself for your actions, understanding that you were in pain and you were doing the best you could?

That was then, this is now.

two

For well you know that it's a fool who plays it cool by making his world a little colder.

— Paul McCartney/John Lennon,
"Hey Jude"

Why Do I Need to be Cool?

This is borderline embarrassing.

That I, a sixty-year-old woman, still yearn to be accepted by the cool, popular kids.

But I can't see any other explanation. I have struggled for years to get past that hurdle of thinking I will not be 'cool' unless I can party with the best of them.

I hated those moments of saying no, I couldn't join in for 'just one drink,' or the times I felt the need to excuse myself from work celebrations and employee pub crawls. I would smile wanly as I listened to the banter exchanged the day after, always feeling like an unsociable loser. I still experience shades of FOMO (Fear of Missing Out) when I leave an event early before the 'real party' starts.

Wow.

Even writing about it is humiliating, yet I know I need to put it out there, because if I struggle with this, then others do too.

And maybe you and I and the other 'not-so-cool' kids can hang out and form our own gang, and be cool with *not* being cool.

I'm being facetious about this yet am in full awareness of its painful truth.

I was not an attractive teenager. I had bad eyesight and wore glasses 24/7 until I could afford contact lenses at eighteen. Acne was a constant source of despair and humiliation from about fifteen to fifty-five—no lie. I had severe rosacea in my middle age, and it wasn't until I made some serious emotional shifts and growth that I finally—FINALLY—had clear but severely scarred skin at fifty-five, just in time for the wrinkles to really make their grand entrance.

Being a strong academic student, I was valedictorian of my grade eight graduating class, yet by grade ten I had been initiated into the cool kids' club in high school and partying became my all-time vocation. Screw school, screw the messed-up 'establishment,' screw anything and anyone that tried to tell me what to do. I didn't need any of it.

And top that off with being in a strict all-girls Catholic high school—I hated it all and was getting out to make my own way as soon as I could. When I graduated from grade twelve with a 60% average in business courses, I vowed I'd never step back into an educational institution.

Ah, the all-knowing folly of youth. . .

To make a long story short, I spent most of the next ten years partying heavily, moving in and out of menial and boring jobs and basically bouncing off the walls of life until an impaired driving charge cost me my licence for a year and I had no other recourse but to go to university.

Why Do I Need to be Cool?

I love when the Universe smacks us across the side of the head with a "No, you goof—THIS WAY!"

It was the best thing that had happened to me to that point, and I'll always be grateful to the trucker who followed my erratically moving vehicle to a stoplight, came out to my car and took my car keys after having already called the police. Good chance he saved my life and possibly the lives of others.

But back to the idea of 'too cool for school.'

I completed my degree and thoroughly enjoyed my university studies—turns out I liked learning after all. I didn't quit partying though—just couldn't drink and drive. I searched out the 'cool' mature students who cracked open a bottle of wine to prep each essay.

When I became a teacher, the 'cool' quotient again kicked in. First of all, I felt I really needed to hide my past from most of these 'straight' toe-the-line educators, who definitely were NOT cool, because truthfully, I felt inferior. It took about half my teaching career before I felt I truly belonged. And I must say that it helped when, after eleven years in the elementary panel, I transferred to teaching secondary, and it was there that I did find my people, my teaching tribe. High school teachers are definitely way more cool—ha! No offence meant to other teaching panels, and I have the utmost respect for the elementary teachers guiding those young learners in socially acceptable behaviours and routines. But I believe the experiences in dealing with teenagers and connecting with them and engaging them requires some involvement and understanding and stepping into their culture. There is a wider cross-section of personality types in high school teachers, given the different areas of expertise needed, and a more open acceptance of individuality; at least, that was my experience.

The crucial a-ha here though is that it's not about being cool or feeling accepted or—god forbid—superior.

I felt so *inferior*, so much less-than, so much of an impostor. And I wasn't. But that bad-person mindset never lets up. My ego, always ready to trip me up and keep me where I was, was the one telling me it's cool to party, it's cool to be the teacher who (secretly) smokes pot. So what if I couldn't control it? (Actually, I could control when I chose to partake, and during my teaching career, that was only on weekends. I definitely could not have managed presenting anything coherent with an alcohol or pot hangover. But Friday at 5:00? Bring on the weekend!) If I didn't indulge, I was like those other nerds who don't know how to let loose and have fun.

You mean those nerds who've been successful in achieving higher education or really useful post-secondary skills and have great careers and are responsible contributors to society and are raising well-balanced children who don't have substance abusers as role models? *Those* nerds?

Oh.

It took decades for me to change that mindset and to recognize how cool it is to be straight. The more time I spent with people who could have fun without getting drunk, who celebrated without intoxicants, who realized that the true highs were never created by drugs, the more I grew to admire them and want to be a part of their social circle. And in the beginning, many of these role models were in recovery of some sort themselves, yet were way ahead of me on their walk. I wanted to emulate their calm confidence and self-discipline.

I began to see how strong you need to be in order to get through the pitfalls and emotional turbulence of life without needing to escape or numb your pain. That those people who were truly achieving some happiness and order and equanimity and fulfillment within their lives without the aid of stimulants or substances were truly the cool crowd. Granted, there are many, many people who are able to manage their appetites and compulsions and enjoy a drink or two or a moderate intake of marijuana to soften the edge without turning it into a no-holds-back bender. But too often the stimulants and intoxicants are a crutch, especially to those of us whose more-is-better switch is broken, and those of us who are uncomfortable in social situations and need something to boost us and raise our 'coolness' factor.

It is so cool to be good within yourself, as you are, fully aware and present, even when it is painful, even when you're struggling. That is the cool crowd.

That's the gang I want to join.

Reflection

Position yourself comfortably in your quiet space. If writing appeals to you, have pen and paper ready, or better yet, a journal.

Close your eyes, and simply focus on your breath. Be aware of breathing in, breathing out, breathing in, breathing out, breathing in, breathing out.

The following questions or statements may be an aid to direct your inner work:

What does 'being cool' mean to you?

How dependent are you on others' opinions of you?

How will you feel if someone you like does not respect your new choices? How will you react?

What choices do you have in your reactions? In your response to this person?

Is this relationship worth going back to the way you've been living?

three

You don't have to control your thoughts.
You just have to stop letting them control you.

— Dan Millman

Mindfulness

I got my first tattoo in my fiftieth year. It was something I'd been thinking of doing for a few years, and hence, had gotten a henna tattoo on my left ankle for the previous two summers so I could try it out to make sure I wanted to permanently ink my body (this was a story and a bit of counsel I loved to share with my high school students: think and plan before you do something relatively irreversible).

Then I waited till my half-century year, as I thought this was an appropriate and monumental milestone worth immortalizing. And the actual tattoo was methodically planned: it had to be a sun symbol, indicating my love of summer, light, positivity, and warmth. Plus a sun symbol is cool, and I wanted a cool tattoo, of course.

But I also wanted it to say something, and I chose the concept of 'freedom,' for many reasons. Turning fifty is often a crucial stepping stone for women, and probably men also. There's something pretty remarkable about hitting that half-century mark, and it has an effect in different ways. For me it was a bit of a 'Fuck you' in the most positive sense. It's that moment when you give your head a shake and say, "Wait a minute... fifty?! How much time have I got left? The rest of it is gonna be about me, or at least a good chunk of it. Fuck you!" I think it's a pretty common reaction and attitude readjustment, especially for women. For the most part, women are the caregivers. If you are a mother then you've most likely experienced years of putting your children's needs before your own. And for some of us, we may have spent years taking care of a partner's needs. Hence, the freedom of the 'Fuck you'!

Anyway, the funniest part of this story (that I also loved to share with my high school students) is that I chose a cursive kanji representation of freedom to be in the middle of my sun symbol. The tattoo looks like this:

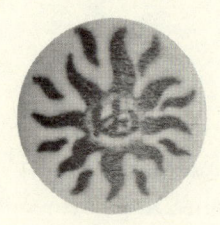

Cool, huh? Well, I found out after the fact that the cursive kanji for freedom actually has two parts to it, and I had chosen only the bottom image:

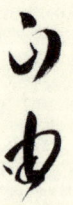

So I've never known if I chose the 'free' or the 'dom' (or is it dumb...)

My students always liked that one.

Yup, we teachers tell the same stories, class after class, semester after semester, year after year. . .

So why did I want freedom? And freedom from what? For one, I was unhappy in my marriage, but it wasn't only that.

Though I couldn't articulate it at the time, I wanted freedom from the thinking patterns that were imprisoning me and causing me so much unhappiness. It wasn't until I became involved in a weekly Vipassana meditation course that I started to see this more clearly, that I realized that developing mindfulness would be my ticket to freedom.

Vipassana is a Pali word and can be translated as 'insight'; a clear awareness of exactly what is happening as it happens. It means to see things as they really are, not as we want them to be or as we think they should be, but as they are.

It is a way of self-transformation through self-observation, and focuses on a deep interconnection between mind and body. There are various interpretations and practices based on Vipassana, but a common result is heightened awareness, or mindfulness.

As I became more and more aware of my own thinking processes and patterns and really started listening to the persistent and insistent chatter going on in my mind, I was shocked to realize what a resentful, bitter and unhappy person was living inside of me. I had a fairly optimistic and happy-enough face that I presented to the world, and I worked in a very social profession where I needed to actively engage what was often a disinterested and inattentive audience of teenagers; I mean, I had to compete with social media and their phones in their hands 24/7. So I saw myself as a fairly upbeat personality handling a full-time career, raising children and managing a household. . . but let's not forget the substance abuse that helped me manage the chaos and moods and stress.

When I first started listening to myself, it was a crucial awakening. I realized how unhappy I was, and it was the first step in making some life-shifting changes. That initial weekly meditation class was helpful, but it was only the first nudge to awareness.

A couple years later, and many years after quitting alcohol, I chose to stop smoking weed as I was organizing a year-long teaching exchange in Australia, and I knew I couldn't be taking my habit with me. I'd been in marriage counselling for years previously, but then switched to another counsellor whose expertise was in addiction. This wonderful woman was pivotal in my changes at that time. She had also practiced mindfulness and meditation extensively throughout her life, so we resonated on many levels (and are still good friends to this day).

Quitting marijuana the year before the exchange was like stepping out of a fog. What awareness had come to me previously was minor compared to the difference in having a clear mind and body. I am not against marijuana at all. I think it has really beneficial medicinal properties and truly has been instrumental for me and some of my friends in coping with stress and anxiety and undiagnosed ADHD. In my case it always became detrimental due to my overuse (again, the broken more-is-better switch).

As far as the practice of Vipassana, though, marijuana and other intoxicants do alter and distort reality, even as a positive shift by simply relaxing a stressed state.

I have chosen and am now choosing to be in my reality at all times, as it is, to the best of my ability. If I wish to progress on a path of increasing mindfulness and self-awareness, I need to be straight and clear at all times, through all situations and interactions. Granted, I still choose to consume caffeine (I love love LOVE my morning coffee) and I enjoy sweets and sugar-infused treats, which some will say changes your state of mind. I'm not disputing any of this, but I choose to avoid intoxicants of any kind.

Being mindful continues to actuate more appreciation of the moment, more engagement in interactions, more involvement in whatever it is that I am doing.

A few years ago, my brother introduced me to the work of Shinzen Young, an American mindfulness teacher and neuroscience research consultant who has developed a systematic approach to categorizing, adapting and teaching meditation known as Unified Mindfulness. He offers multiple retreats, both residential and virtual, in the United States, and a week-long retreat each spring and fall in Ontario, Canada. I had the opportunity to attend one of these at that time, and it was an integral and shifting step in my meditation practice and mindfulness journey. In his book, *The Science of Enlightenment*, Shinzen speaks of how focused mindfulness and meditation can 'add years' to your life experience:

> If I told you there's a process that would require ten minutes of your time each day for the rest of your life, and if you do this process, it is likely to add sixty years to your lifespan, you would probably say that that was a good deal. Now imagine that you will live just a normal number of years, but that your experience of each moment will be twice as full as it currently is; that is, the scale at which you live each moment will be doubled. If you only lived for sixty years, but lived each moment twice as fully as the ordinary person lives it, that would be the equivalent of one hundred twenty years of richesse. Not a bad deal. . . Meditation is the key to this kind of nonmythical life extension. The central feature of any meditation system from anywhere around the world is that, by developing an extraordinary degree of focus and presence, it allows you to live your life two or three hundred percent 'bigger.' (Young 31 – 32)

My life continues to feel bigger and fuller and richer. I have fewer and fewer regrets because more often than not, I follow what I know to be true and right for me and make the effort to choose wisely in my interactions with others for our mutual benefit.

When you take that first step in really listening to what you're saying to yourself, you may be surprised to find what you are feeding your inner dragons.

Reflection

Position yourself comfortably in your quiet space. If writing appeals to you, have pen and paper ready, or better yet, a journal.

Close your eyes, and simply focus on your breath. Be aware of breathing in, breathing out, breathing in, breathing out, breathing in, breathing out.

The following questions or statements may be an aid to direct your inner work:

Sit quietly in awareness first of your breath, in and out, then become aware of whatever is going on in your mind. Allow its expression with no judgement or control or revision; simply listen to what it is saying.

At various points during your day, take time to stop and listen, really listen, to the constant chatter going on in your mind. Do this especially when you are feeling down or low, because most likely you are talking yourself further into this frame of mind.

A good exercise at these times is to take pen and paper and write from 'stream of consciousness' (every single thought written as it comes to mind with no thought of grammar, spelling or structure, and especially with no judgement).

Mindfulness

If you have taken the time to write down your thoughts, are you now able to rewrite them into something that is contradictory to the negative self-abuse or comparison to others or criticism of others? Can you write these conversations as the kindest person you know would write them?

four

Authentic happiness is always independent of external conditions.

— Epictetus, *The Art of Living*

The Art of Living

Although I have dabbled in various types of meditation most of my life, the life shift I experienced in April 2018—one month before my sixtieth birthday—was monumental. That April, I took my first ten-day Vipassana meditation course in the teachings of Satya Narayan Goenka at the Ontario Vipassana Centre.

This is not a promotional advertisement for this organization and the courses they offer. I have to include it in this narrative, and explain some of the background and basic tenets, because without this experience, this narrative would most likely not exist.

This practice has shown me the "Art of Living"—and I use the quotation marks here as credit to S. N. Goenka, the founder of the Vipassana tradition I now follow. He describes this practice as learning the Art of Living, which interestingly corresponds with the quote at the beginning of this chapter.

In the 1950s, Goenka, a successful businessman in Burma, began his journey in the practice of Vipassana. Unable to find a cure for his migraine headaches despite consulting medical practitioners across the globe, it was suggested by a friend that he try a ten-day meditation course by Sayagyi U Ba Khin that could possibly help him alleviate the pain. Having exhausted all other options, he decided to give it a try, and not only did the practice relieve him of the migraines, it was the beginning of a life-long vocation of teaching and a world-wide organization that now has over 180 centres offering these courses all year long, absolutely free of charge.

Once you have completed a ten-day program, you are welcome to donate, within your means and volition, so that future students can benefit from this technique, but no money is accepted beforehand for instruction, meals or accommodation. Each centre is maintained by volunteers who donate their time to serve on courses by preparing meals, cleaning and maintaining residences, etc., so that students can work safely, quietly and uninterrupted throughout the course. I have never witnessed something so wonderfully brilliant, giving and accessible to all. When I finished my first course, I fully expected there to be some kind of persuasive techniques used to drum up donations or service, yet this never happened. It's hard to believe that, in this day and age, centres can exist and flourish by these means, yet they do, and it's one of most wonderful things I have experienced. There are other meditation traditions and facilities which operate in a similar way and it's wonderful to have these practices available to all.

The technique that is being taught is presented as the same meditation practice given by Gautama the Buddha over 2500 years ago, as recorded in the suttas (teachings and discourses), and most particularly in the Satipatthana Sutta. It is not Buddhism; Siddhartha Gautama was never a 'Buddhist.' That sect was originated by later followers.

What is taught and practised is Vipassana, which translates as "meditation involving concentration on the body or its sensations, or the insight which this provides," or "seeing things exactly as they are." In learning to do so, the goal is to develop equanimity (mental calmness) in all situations, and therefore alleviate the suffering that is universal in all humans. We create our suffering in our reactions, in our cravings for things to be different, in our aversion to situations we don't like or want.

Any of this sound familiar in your own personal anguish? It's the classic human condition. And whether or not it is the 'true' teaching of the Buddha, the technique and practice is very often life-shifting.

Vipassana teaches us to become aware of all physical and emotional sensations and reactions. There are three main pillars in this teaching:

Sila – living a life of morality

Samadhi – developing concentration of the mind

Panna – cultivating inner wisdom

Sila is based on five precepts:

1. Abstain from killing any being
2. Abstain from stealing
3. Abstain from all sexual misconduct
4. Abstain from telling lies
5. Abstain from all intoxicants

I am including all of these details to illustrate the steps on my path: within my first year after taking the course, I struggled with only one of these—intoxicants, of course. In his discourses, Goenka addresses this precept and shares stories of people, who, after many years of 'addiction' to alcohol or drugs, lose their attachment to them and are able to live without them.

Shinzen Young (referenced in the previous chapter), a world-renowned American meditation teacher who has practised in various Vipassana traditions, speaks openly of how he ended a ten-year addiction to marijuana after taking this ten-day course in his earlier explorations in meditation.

I lasted two months after my first course. I had gone in after smoking heavily and often for the four years prior, and even more so the three months before the course as I had just retired from teaching. Nothing was holding me back from getting high daily at that time.

I truly felt transformed after that initial course and had no desire to smoke—at first. But then summer hit, and summer means the cottage, and the cottage is *the* ultimate Place of Permission. I think I lasted an hour after I walked in the door... maybe less.

And it didn't take long before it became a daily habit again.

Because I was so moved by the practice and the organization itself, and because I was retired, I began volunteering at the centre one week a month. It started with kitchen service, helping to prepare meals for about one hundred people daily during the courses, and then I began working in the office and helping with registration and various other duties.

One week every month I was clear and straight but going home was another story.

I felt like a hypocrite.

And my suffering was more intense because I was so very aware of it. You can't not know what you know.

I took another ten-day course in January 2019 and went even deeper in my meditation and my experience. I lasted only a month after that one.

From that point on, my determination and quest to come to an understanding of my behaviours and ultimately let go of those which no longer served me, led to the story you now hold in your hands.

I decided my best approach, and what had worked for me in the past, was, as you know by now, to *write my way through it.*

All of this has led me to an understanding and daily practice in the Art of Living. This is the reward of our practice, of our being completely honest with ourselves, of our taking a sincere moral self-inventory and doing something about it, of our being of service to others, of our learning to be the master of our minds, of our living in a perspective of loving kindness to all—including, and foremost, ourselves.

Living in the Flow, living the 'Right Life' for you, is living a blessed and charmed existence, every day, every moment. It doesn't mean everything turns out exactly as you want it to; it means you are good with embracing each moment AS IT IS. Not wanting it to be something else, not worrying about what may or may not happen in the future, not dwelling on what did or didn't happen in the past.

AS IT IS.

I marvel at how big and full and rich my life has become and continues to be—ever bigger, richer and fuller. As Shinzen Young states in *The Science of Enlightenment*:

> Since meditation enhances any life activity, we meditate for ourselves so that we can gain a special kind of strength. We can work more joyously and effectively; we can perform better, we can enjoy our meal more fully, we can enjoy music more, and there is a general elevation of pleasure in life. (Young 40)

This abundance in experience can be yours. But each step must also be yours. And your experience will flourish accordingly with the steps you take.

My way, my steps, my path are my own. They may not work for you. Take from my story what does work, and begin your journey, forging your path toward real happiness and liberation.

And release your dragons. Let them go to wherever dragons need to go, and begin to reap the treasure they have been hiding from you.

Dragons love to fly; allow them their freedom, and in doing so you will tap into your own.

Reflection

Position yourself comfortably in your quiet space. If writing appeals to you, have pen and paper ready, or better yet, a journal.

Close your eyes, and simply focus on your breath. Be aware of breathing in, breathing out, breathing in, breathing out, breathing in, breathing out.

The following questions or statements may be an aid to direct your inner work:

Is there something you've been yearning to do, daydreaming about being able to do for your own personal growth when you have the time/money/right circumstances?

Think of all the reasons why this isn't a good time.

Then think of all the reasons why you should do it now or as soon as possible.

Go back to your list of 'can'ts' and create possibilities to work through each one.

five

Every difficulty in life presents us with an opportunity to turn inward and to invoke our own submerged inner resources. The trials we endure can and should introduce us to our strengths.

– Epictetus, *The Art of Living*

The Gift of the Gobsmack

Gobsmacked = utterly astonished, astounded.

Gob = a lump or clot of a slimy or viscous substance.

What a fantastic word! It's visceral—not only is it cacophonous and harsh to your ears, but being smacked by a gob?! Yuck! Best word ever.

I know that the word 'gob' comes from the Irish and Scottish Gaelic slang for mouth, but I prefer my version.

But the funny thing is, when I first heard it, I thought it was 'godsmacked,' and I loved that even more.

To be smacked by God—what a gift! That 'He' would take the time to reach down and give you one across the side of the head when you're off track and doing something stupid or detrimental to your purpose. Beautiful.

And that is what it is, isn't it? I'm sure you can think of at least one—if not many—times in your life when something occurred that smacked you right off the track you were on, because basically you had no choice.

The times when 'fate' or 'destiny' or 'the universe' or 'God'—some higher power—stepped in and took the wheel because you definitely needed a drastic change in direction.

These gobsmacked moments are often seen as calamitous tragedies when they occur. They could be an accident out of the blue, could be the loss of a job, could be a stupid decision while under the influence that has serious repercussions; something BIG happens to smack you across the head and wake you up and out of that present trajectory.

And it's painful! And shocking, and not at all pleasant.

One of my biggest gobsmacks was losing my licence while driving impaired in my twenties. A bad choice made while under the influence that looked like a calamity and huge setback at the time, but was in reality a boon, a positive push in a completely different direction. And a humbling and painful inventory of the self, to boot.

Initially, after being gobsmacked, we're thoroughly pissed at Life and raging at our misfortune.

But once you start clearing your sense organs in order to breathe—because it can knock the breath right out of you—you start seeing and listening and noticing where you're at and where you've been headed. Once the raging is over, and if you're open to learning from Life's lessons, you start examining why this may have happened to you, why your actions have culminated in this painful punch.

Yes, we are the creators of our circumstances; we have built the house of our present situations.

And yes, it's much easier to view these difficult occurrences from the victim mindset: "I don't deserve this!" "Those bastards fired me!"

"Why did she have to leave me?" We often strike out at whomever or whatever we see as the perpetrators of this injustice, because then we don't have to look at ourselves.

There can be justified feelings of unfairness, and there can be offenders enacting their own misguided intentions, but regardless, it happened to you, and you still need to deal with the fallout. Blaming something or someone else does not move you forward or present opportunity for personal growth.

That's *their* business, not yours. Your business is you.

You are the only one who can rebuild your house.

You are the original architect, framer, mason. When you're gobsmacked by a tsunami of circumstance, you are also the one who chooses and creates the extent of the damage, and the only one who can manifest the rebuilding. We can help each other and get guidance and support from each other, but the internal growth is solely our own.

It's both a blessing and a burden.

And there's another side to being gobsmacked, if we look at the "godsmacked" version.

Sometimes we are blessed with a fortuitous turn of events, an unexpected unforeseen situation that brings good fortune and causes a pronounced positive life shift.

Taking my first Vipassana course in the Goenka tradition was an unambiguous godsmack. It smacked me so thoroughly that I seemed to crack open, in a really good way. I believe it was the ten days of silence which allowed me to spend undistracted time within myself that was the crucial stimulus. That redefined the course of my life and was such a clear indication of my purpose from that moment on.

I've found that responding to the gobsmack or the godsmack and really looking and listening to its message can create a regenerative flow in your life. You're no longer swimming upstream, in great resistance, fighting for how you think things should be rather than allowing Life to show you your best way. You become more in tune with your inner wisdom, that undeniable feeling of 'knowing' which way to proceed when making decisions.

You start enjoying the resonance of right living rather than always hitting the discord of opposition.

Being godsmacked can allow your life to become less of a battleground and more like a garden; one where you accept and learn from the gifts each season brings and you reap the harvest of what you've sowed.

Look for your gobsmacks and your godsmacks. Heed their message. Be grateful for the 'tough love' that may give you necessary redirection towards a richer and more harmonious life.

Reflection

Position yourself comfortably in your quiet space. If writing appeals to you, have pen and paper ready, or better yet, a journal.

Close your eyes, and simply focus on your breath. Be aware of breathing in, breathing out, breathing in, breathing out, breathing in, breathing out.

The following questions or statements may be an aid to direct your inner work:

The Gift of the Gobsmack

Think of an event that seemed to be a tragedy at the time. Think of all the pain you felt and struggles it caused.

What positives can you acknowledge from it? What did you learn? What were you able to change?

Was it avoidable? Given the opportunity to relive it, what would you change about the event or its repercussions?

Sacred Path Card #44
Sacred Space

The Sacred Space card insists on respect for the possessions, ideas, homes and persons of others. This also applies to demanding it for the Self. Respect yourself so that others will see that reflection in themselves and in how they deal with you. Be willing to say no.

Sacred Space means that you consider your body, feelings, and possessions sacred and will not allow others to abuse them. Only invite those who have earned the right into your Sacred Space. You are the one who sets up how other people treat you through how you treat yourself.

In all cases the respect you show yourself and other life-forms determines how you relate to the Planetary Family. If you allow others to be destructive in your Sacred Space, on some level you don't have the guts to be disliked. It is not important to be liked by others, but it is important to be able to live with yourself. Happiness begins within. (Sams 323)

six

Shame corrodes the very part of us that believes we are capable of change.

– Brené Brown, *I Thought It Was Just Me*

I'm a Bad Person

Guilt and shame are familiar allies in the addict's compulsive behaviour framework. Having been raised Roman Catholic, they were a part of my psyche pretty much since inception, I think; that lovely concept of 'Original Sin'—born with a black mark on your soul, doomed to be bad from the beginning.

The "I'm a bad person" self-concept is recognizable in many people with compulsive behaviours and/or addictions. Because there is so much shame associated with these behaviours and what appears to be an inability to control undesirable reactions and patterns, we default to considering ourselves 'bad' people. We know, based on previous outcomes, that one drink often leads to far too many drinks which leads to regrets for things said, actions taken or abuse in a variety of forms. We know that a little smoke of marijuana often leads to a repeat performance of a blotto evening of more smoking, vegging in front of a screen and non-stop stuffing your face.

We know this and yet, we reach for the drink or the joint because that conniving and immoral voice within tells us it will be different this time: "Just have one, or okay maybe two, and you know how lovely that initial buzz is. Don't you want that? Of course you do. Go ahead, just one—it will feel *so* good." Or sometimes the voice tells us: "Everyone else is doing it and having fun—you can too! It's just a party; you *deserve* to have fun! Why deprive yourself?" That voice—the ego—is merciless, unscrupulous and only out for its survival.

You do it again. . .and again. . .and again. . . with the same outcome of remorse and recrimination and self-abnegation, feeling awful mentally, emotionally and physically and wondering how and if your poor body will recover from this one.

Those thousands of mornings, that instant of despairing and disgusted consciousness, painfully piecing together what you can remember from the previous evening, not wanting to open your eyes and face the day, unable to stop or ignore the inner tirade of abuse, again, and again. . .

You MUST be a bad person.

Otherwise you would be able to stop this revolting behaviour.

Otherwise you wouldn't have this 'problem.'

Otherwise you'd make good, positive choices that didn't harm you or your relationships.

We all have different reasons why our compulsive behaviours start in the first place, and I'm not discounting the evidence towards alcoholism, in particular, being possibly genetic and chemically triggered. Many of us know that one drink is never one drink. As for the physical withdrawal symptoms, however, I had never experienced any when cold-turkey quitting alcohol or marijuana. What I did suffer through was the loss and void of my familiar support and the compelling craving for what I knew and thought I 'loved.'

I'm a Bad Person

I was a bad person because I kept returning to that 'love' that was mine alone, that familiar friend I could cuddle up with for that lovely numbing comfort. Each time I returned, it never took very long—maybe a month—before I was down the same rabbit-hole of compulsive, self-abusive behaviours and that familiar remorse and shame.

No wonder I felt like a bad person.

And after those first or second or fortieth attempts at 'stopping,' I became a master of secrecy and deception. I had to hide my relapse from those close to me because of my shame.

One of the most painful repercussions of these behaviours is the guilt and shame we become mired in, much of it self-imposed, and much of it bestowed by others who are trying to survive in the wake of our chaos and variability. If you're anything like I was, you may see yourself as a Jekyll and Hyde character with contradictory attributes to each state of mind. Yet within each personality, you feel completely comfortable in being that person at that time, which leads to confusion and self-abnegation and layers of self-abuse. We are masters at magnifying our own levels of guilt and these then are often compounded by the recriminations from those closest to us, often justified, and often a result of their own triggers.

Being raised as a Catholic, I am an expert on guilt, both in the receiving and the imposing. As I grew more mindful, and most particularly in the raising of my children, I became aware of the manipulative dangers of both sides of this destructive strategy. I was raised on it, and I used it, and it's no surprise that I attracted partners who were adept in its application, usually using it to keep me 'in my place' and maintain their status quo. If you're in a relationship that has become co-dependent, as is quite common with alcoholics and those dependent on drugs, a partner can become quite adept at triggering your low self-esteem if things aren't going their way. A quick stab about how "you'll never change" can quickly deflate any attempts at growth or shifts within the relationship.

Given that we dwell in the "I'm a bad person" syndrome, guilt is embraced by our self-serving egos to continue feeding our low self-concept. We expect it, we bow down to our 'deserved' punishments and when our partner or friend has reached the end of their tirade, we finish it off within ourselves until we're a broken mess, or a blotto mess—which generally happens in time. What better way to escape that self-abasement than to amplify it with excesses of our comforting substance of choice?

The vicious circle continues.

The guilt and shame play off each other:

> Guilt is a natural feeling that can result following a poor choice or a mistake. Feelings of guilt stem from our moral conscience and let us know we've done something that violates our moral compass or "right vs. wrong." . . . On the other hand, shame is a feeling of inadequacy. With shame, you may feel like simple mistakes are a sign that you're defective as a person or that you're incompetent. . .While guilt can give you motivation to correct your mistake or error in behavior, shame keeps you in a mindset of self-loathing. Guilt pushes you to connect with others in order to repair the wrong, while shame causes you to hide from others in order to minimize the embarrassment you feel. **Whereas guilt is a judgement about your behavior, shame is a judgement about yourself.** (Verta Health)

No wonder we feel like a bad person.

If you're like me, you blame yourself for returning again and again to that which you know, that which has given you comfort in the past and has helped you to deal with pain and discomfort and difficult situations.

There is a reason why it all began. And that doesn't make you a bad person.

It makes you someone who has not known or been shown how to deal with pain in more healthy and constructive ways. It makes you someone who has learned a coping mechanism that has served you in the past. Now it no longer serves you. You serve it, and it has become your master—but only if you allow it.

There is always a choice in every situation, in every moment, in every thought.

And THOUGHT is the crucial and life-shifting word here. It is our thinking that creates and reinforces and feeds our habit patterns, and these become ingrained like ruts that we are unable to steer ourselves from or avoid.

But this does NOT make you a bad person.

This means that you need to look very carefully at the thinking patterns that have brought you to this place and to examine how these behaviours have served you in the past. Are those reasons still there? If so, would it make sense to find alternative, less damaging and more supportive assists to work through the issues, the pain, the discomfort you have been numbing or attempting to escape?

This journey of life is an incredibly difficult and painful experience and many of us do not have the love and support to help us navigate through it. Ultimately we are all on our own, forging our own journey, making decisions based on our own perspectives. No one else can take the steps for us, even though there are many enabling parents and partners who—with the best of intentions—try to *fix* everything for their kids or mates. It is fundamentally a growth process we each own and are responsible for. And it's hard, and it hurts—a lot. There are all kinds of ways you can distract yourself, avoid the pain, escape the reality, numb the discomfort—at least for a while.

These do not make you a bad person.

If these behaviours continue and start causing you grief and shame and remorse and become detrimental to you and your relationships, then it may be time to take a searching and fearless moral inventory (or as I say, "look your shit in the face") and do something about it.

You may need some help and support through this process, because change is *never* easy. It's incredibly painful and difficult for most of us and so very easy to fall back into our ruts at the slightest nudge. It's very scary to willingly choose to face our triggers and the pain we've suppressed for so long.

If you feel that you have unresolved issues from your past or present that are causing your difficulties, you may choose to find a professional therapist. Throughout my life I have had years of counselling—through my bout with bulimia, then through twelve of the eighteen years of my difficult marriage, then near the end of my marriage as I struggled with my abuse of marijuana.

I believe that counselling is one of the most courageous steps we can take in our personal growth and life journeys. It's easy to continue the distractions that can (more or less) keep us surviving and getting to the next day, but it takes courage to be willing and open to face your personal minefield and deal with it, and many of us can only do so with the help of a trained professional.

I have the highest regard for people in that profession. What an honourable vocation—no less than that of a medical practitioner who helps to cure and sustain our bodies. Equally as important are those caring, compassionate, listening souls who work together with us to gently unravel the convoluted chaos of our emotions and triggers and wounds, and hold us on our journey to heal.

It all won't go away on its own. Habits and thinking patterns become ingrained because most of us drastically dislike change, and our ego loves nothing more than to avoid the discomfort of change.

And yet, CHANGE IS THE ONLY CONSTANT.

Nothing lasts forever, nothing remains the same—not mountains, not oceans, not people, not the blood in our veins or the breath in our body. Everything changes, every moment.

An acceptance of this is a key component in coming out of the 'bad person' syndrome. Whatever your past behaviours and outcomes, whatever your past regrets and remorse, you CAN make a change. You CAN rewire your thinking patterns, you CAN release that dragon that hoards your truths, you CAN unfetter that inner abuser who keeps telling you it's not possible.

And yet even that inner abuser has served you in your journey to this point. You have survived; you've made it this far and you're looking for help because it's no longer serving you. Rather than continue in the well of shame, thinking you need to cut this blight, cut this festering thinking, out of your being, recognize what it has given you in the past. Embrace it for having served you. This inner abuser is how you coped and survived for a long time, maybe decades. It *has* served you, and now, you no longer need it. Release that 'bad person' voice within. Release it with gratitude.

YOU are not a bad person.

Reflection

Position yourself comfortably in your quiet space. If writing appeals to you, have pen and paper ready, or better yet, a journal.

Close your eyes, and simply focus on your breath. Be aware of breathing in, breathing out, breathing in, breathing out, breathing in, breathing out.

The following questions or statements may be an aid to direct your inner work:

List all the reasons why you think you are a bad person.

Beside each of these, can you list the reasons why these behaviours or situations happened? And can you do so without adding shame or guilt onto them? Just be as objective as possible in detailing what motivated these, as though they belong to someone else. See the pain and the struggle of that 'other person' and give empathy and compassion to him or her for the choices that were triggered by pain and unconscious reactions.

Can you find it in yourself to forgive yourself for those decisions?

seven

There are those people who can eat one piece of chocolate, one piece of cake, drink one glass of wine. There are even people who smoke one or two cigarettes a week. And then there are people for whom one of anything is not even an option.

— Abigail Thomas, *Thinking About Memoir*

The More-is-Better Switch

A dear friend coined the "broken more-is-better switch" regarding my life-long behaviours when we reconnected in our mid-fifties and became partners, post-separation from our former spouses. He'd known me throughout many of my life stages, and had chosen to end our initial brief relationship in our mid-twenties because of my excessive and irresponsible behaviours. We'd originally met at age eighteen in a meditation group called PSI Mind Development (the 'cult' mentioned previously—more on that later), that, despite its self-implosive demise, was a positive and crucial introduction in my eternal mindfulness and spiritual journey. It's unfortunate that the organization degenerated and then eventually collapsed due to corrupt leadership, but in its initial years there were many positive experiences and teachings. I'd become involved in the group because even at that young age I could see my substance abuse escalating, and I knew my circle of friends at the time would continue to accompany me and cajole me down that path. I needed a change.

In the few years I was an avid participant in the group, I drank very little and shunned all drugs as evil and negative. But upon my escape from its clutches, the first job I landed was a waitressing position in a very trendy and reputable family-owned restaurant, where I continued to work on and off for ten years. I was also trained on bartending and would often work till close.

Ahh. . . 'close' in the restaurant and hospitality business often means 'open' for the staff—that is, the bar, of course. I mean, you've been serving drinks all night to partying people having a great time imbibing, and now it's *your* turn. The alcohol is often free-flowing and after hours, no one's measuring. And drinking-and-driving restrictions and consequences were not as enforced as they are today, unfortunately. Besides, no one's on the road at 4:00 am so you're just going to be hitting the curbs rather than endangering others' lives.

My twenties were definitely the more-is-better years. As another dear drinking buddy of those times liked to say, "If it's good enough to do, it's good enough to overdo." We'd chuckle wryly as we toasted and drank another one. . .

From my first exposure having access to unlimited amounts of alcohol at the age of twelve, I rarely knew the meaning of 'enough' until I was throwing up or blacking out.

If you are someone for whom 'moderation' is a foreign language, then you know exactly what I'm talking about. When your more-is-better switch is broken, it's stuck. More is *always* better. You don't have a rational discernment when it comes to moderating your substance intake; reaching for that first drink or that first toke or that first doughnut inevitably leads to excess and its ramifications.

Those were my drinking days, yet that same behaviour and mindset of having no sense of limits was often present in my use of marijuana

The More-is-Better Switch

and in my relationship with food, especially when I suffered from bulimia briefly in my early twenties. There was always a need to gorge myself with everything.

Why? Why do some of us struggle with a broken more-is-better switch? Society and advertising certainly enable and abet this mindset. More wine, more weed, more food, more gambling, more shopping, more renovating, more, more, more! We are sold on the misconception that these things will enhance our experience, will improve our sexual attraction, will boost our confidence, will help us attain that elusive 'happiness' and avoid the inherent struggle of reality.

And for those of us with the broken switch, we don't have a concept of 'enough'; most often the only reason we stop is because we pass out, we black out, we've depleted our savings.

Why can't we stop ourselves?

I've asked myself this question for decades and I believe that it all begins with numbing our pain, our discomfort, our anxiety, our social awkwardness; whatever it is that isn't feeling good at the time. This is the 'comfort' (and I use that term ironically) that I would get from my extreme excesses—a mind-numbing, blotto, vegging stupor, oblivion—but no pain. . .until tomorrow. And the tomorrows are so incredibly painful.

There are reasons why we choose these behaviours, again and again, and it's not because we are bad people. We are in pain, and to this point, this is how we have managed our pain and continued to get through each day and each situation, to continue putting one foot in front of the other, to continue to survive. We *have* survived.

If you have picked up this book, you know that this method of survival is no longer working for you. It's far more detrimental and dangerous than helpful and comforting.

Or, like me, you may be at a point where your life is quite good, really good, better than it's ever been, and you're still struggling with your broken more-is-better switch. If we are truly happy and are living our 'best' life, why is this still an issue? Why is our switch still stuck?

Either way, it means it may be time for a change, and it may be time to look outside yourself, for someone, preferably a professional or a community organization, who can help you to look within. It can be very difficult, especially at the start, to really see the beliefs we have held on to and nurtured that have brought us to this place.

I am forever grateful to those individuals who have been such an integral part of my journey, in helping me see the reasons for my triggers and my broken switch. And though we truly are solely responsible for ourselves and our choices and our self-talk and our reactions to others (no matter what we see them as inflicting upon us), it is so very helpful and comforting to have those individuals to hold us up when we break down in the realizations of our concealed and painful psychological imbalances, and to help us take each step as we climb out of the well of grief or anger or hatred or fear or despair—or all of the above.

The letting go of these thought patterns is completely up to each one of us, but we have lived with and nurtured our deceptive dragons for so long that we believe their stories, and are not sure what would be left of us without them. A good therapist or a supportive community group can help us see through the mindsets we have created and fed to what lies under them, in order to help us release these familiar misconceptions to find our stronger and clearer selves within.

Releasing those dragons does not mean there will be a void or an emptiness; there can be instead a calm and a sense of fulfillment and a new and more complete appreciation of yourself and your journey.

Reflection

Position yourself comfortably in your quiet space. If writing appeals to you, have pen and paper ready, or better yet, a journal.

Close your eyes, and simply focus on your breath. Be aware of breathing in, breathing out, breathing in, breathing out, breathing in, breathing out.

The following questions or statements may be an aid to direct your inner work:

Scarcity and abundance—have you always had enough, in reality, even when you were fearful of being deprived?

Many of us who react through excess do not do so due to a lack of sustenance in our past, but to fill an emotional void. What are you needing to fill? What are you choosing to push down, to stuff, to suppress?

What are you having difficulty letting go of? And who would you be if you no longer had that behaviour, that belief?

eight

Our culture made a virtue of living only as extroverts. We discouraged the inner journey, the quest for a center. So we lost our center and have to find it again.

— Anaïs Nin

To thine own self be true.

— William Shakespeare, *Hamlet*

The Pull to Hibernate

One of the guiltiest pleasures and indulgences within my compulsive behaviour patterns has been the craving to stay home alone for an evening, a day, or a couple of days with my substance of choice in full supply and very little probability of interruption. Hence, the cottage—the ultimate Place of Permission and unrestrained retreat. Hole up in your cozy cabin stocked up with all your favorite indulgences and munchies and enter the world of la-la-land.

It was the one place that I tried to avoid during my times of abstinence, and the one place that could often trigger the nosedive off the wagon.

When my children were both on their own and I lived alone in my later fifties, my home also became that place of permission. But I could not 'avoid' my home, so, when I was ready to face my dragons and not drown them in alcohol, my home also became my place of process, my safe haven. I could shut the door, turn off the phone and allow myself to dig deep and trudge through the mire of my wounds and triggers, painfully forging new paths that did not follow the habitual ruts I had previously paced and pounded to bleak perfection.

At first, I couldn't stay home alone. I was afraid to face the triggers, so I filled my time and created social engagements as distractions. But I always found that I had about a two-hour max in my social interactions limit when I was straight. And by social engagements, I mean events where there were groups of people and the exchanges were often fairly light and superficial. I've since discovered that 'small talk' is a bane of the introvert, and that introverts often need to recharge in solitude after group social events. It was quite a revelation, when as a middle-aged adult I realized how much I resonated with this personality type. How could that be? I'd always been the life of the party, the one to stay till the bitter end (or my own bitter end of passing out), the one ready for a spontaneous outing or adventure.

Because I'd started drinking and partying early in my teens, I don't think I ever gave myself the opportunity to truly know who and how I was. I was too preoccupied with escaping my pain, with fitting in with the cool kids, with proving my popularity. I didn't realize until much later that alcohol was providing my voice in most social situations, and that much of what it was saying was not who I really was.

Any time I spent alone during my earlier drinking years was usually either with a couple bottles of wine, or in the anguish of remorse, unable to face others due to the physical and emotional repercussions of the night before and/or the self-loathing of the morning after.

The Pull to Hibernate

I didn't really like being alone and by myself until my fifties and sixties, until I separated and realized how much I enjoyed living alone—with furry companions. Never underestimate the unconditional love of your dog. My Kaya helped me so, so much in working through those times when I needed to be without human company.

What is an introvert? Some definitions include the words 'shy' and 'reticent.' I don't feel I'm either of those. Many definitions include the ideas of preferring calm, minimally stimulating environments and needing to recharge by spending time alone after socializing. That is quite true in my case. I'm not a risk-taker (at least, not anymore, and that may simply be due to the sober realization of impending mortality) but I love multitasking, which is apparently more of an extrovert quality. We all have bits and pieces of both extremes within.

I love these clarifications from *Quiet* by Susan Cain:

> Introverts. . . may have strong social skills and enjoy parties and business meetings, but after a while wish they were home in their pyjamas. They prefer to devote their social energies to close friends, colleagues, and family. They listen more than they talk, think before they speak, and often feel as if they express themselves better in writing than in conversation. They tend to dislike conflict. Many have a horror of small talk, but enjoy deep discussions. . . The word *introvert* is not a synonym for hermit or misanthrope. (Cain 11)

When I finally embraced my introvert nature, so much made sense. Life and being straight became so much easier. It also helped that I'd entered the "fuck it fifties" when you realize you couldn't care less what most people think of you. Your children, your partner, your close friends—yes, you value their opinions because you love them and, for the most part, you appreciate their insight and perspectives.

But otherwise—hell no. You see that life is too short to live by others' standards, and you see that the whole party/social scene can be such an empty interaction and distraction. I'd always known that I hated 'small talk' but thought there was something wrong with me, that I felt less than others (which I did) and that I did not have enough information to intelligently contribute to political and state-of-the-world discussions (which I didn't).

But I realized that these were not issues or ideas or exchanges that I cared about; I didn't want to keep up with the latest news or the newest trends or the hottest topics. Small talk makes you feel *smaller*. You stumble through and laugh with the empty witticisms forced into the void of conversation. . . as you continue to shrink.

So, rather than feel badly about myself because I truly did not enjoy these situations, I either stopped going or made arrangements to only attend on *my* time. I found a couple hours was a reasonable and enjoyable amount of time to see who I wanted to see and say what I wanted to say, to enjoy people's company and then to gracefully make my departure without offending well-meaning friends and without inflicting discomfort on myself.

I am an introvert, and a very happy one. I love deeply personal one-on-one conversations with people I enjoy, and I'm always grateful to have coffee with those who may need a sounding board, as I usually gain much also.

And I love my hibernation times. Staying home alone for an evening with my favourite TV shows and yummy snacks always makes me feel warm and cozy and replenished, and ready then to extend myself out to the world, if necessary, the next day. I no longer feel guilty for my pleasure in binging Netflix or feel the need to be contributing and extending myself more so than not, and most particularly when I know I'm at my saturation point. I now honour those times whenever possible.

In the past, my substance of choice would alter or distort my reality and perspective, and it was in this state that I could give myself 'permission' to hibernate, to munch out, to not give a shit for the moment. Now, I give myself fully aware permission when I so choose, and these are no longer my 'guilty' pleasures. This fulfills my need to pull back from the demands and chaos and distractions and barrage of society and tune it out, and that's okay. There is no guilt involved. And I am not advocating full-on excesses in these behaviours—the goal is moderation at all costs (see what I did there. . .).

Enjoy your 'vegging' time, your alone time; embrace it, allow it, and keep in mind that you also honour the amazing organism that is your body, this miraculous vessel that houses your spirit.

And honour your introvert self, no matter where you are in the spectrum of needing alone time. Enjoy your own company. Be your own best friend. Laugh with and at yourself, talk to yourself (maybe just in the privacy of your home), write to yourself, dance with yourself, do the things that bring you joy and calm and regeneration, even if they aren't the 'perfect' and 'most beneficial' physically or mentally. We're not 'perfect' all the time, and yet we're exactly our own personal perfect and exactly our own personal truth—ALL the time.

Reflection

Position yourself comfortably in your quiet space. If writing appeals to you, have pen and paper ready, or better yet, a journal.

Close your eyes, and simply focus on your breath. Be aware of breathing in, breathing out, breathing in, breathing out, breathing in, breathing out.

The following questions or statements may be an aid to direct your inner work:

What does spending time alone look like for you? How would you like it to look?

What scares you about spending time alone?

What steps can you take to make your alone time nurturing and restorative? How can you 'treat' yourself healthfully in your alone time?

nine

Extremes are easy. Strive for balance.

— Colin Wright

Highs / Lows

There have been many times in my life when I've been an overachiever, always needing to get things DONE, and DONE WELL and ON TIME—no, BEFORE the deadline (because I cannot handle the anxiety of being late). And on those occasions when I was responsible for the outcome of an event, either for personal friends or professional development, my anxiety would be through the roof as, of course, the whole thing relied on ME. I was ultimately responsible for its failure or success.

And if it 'failed' in any way, the only thought in mind was how quickly I could get to that first drink or drug or bag of Doritos to numb my pain and suffering and disappointment in myself.

It made sense that I needed to stop the pain.

And if it was a great success, the only thought in mind was how quickly I could get to that first drink or drug or bag of Doritos to toast my achievement and celebrate the high.

We also have a need to stop the pleasure.

Huh?

Those intense moments of 'bliss' and self-adulation can be as detrimental as the downside, and this became viscerally apparent to me during one of my ten-day Vipassana retreats of silent meditation.

I was sitting on my bed in my residence at one of the tea breaks, quietly processing as I did each day at that time. This time, the entire hour became overtaken by an overwhelming feeling of happiness and rapture and huge gratitude for the opportunities I had been given within my practice and service at the centre, and for the lovely individuals who were now my tribe, my sangha, my community; for the turn my life had taken and for the possibilities ahead in the path I was choosing to walk.

All good things—all great, wonderful choices and situations—and I sobbed and reveled in it all for an hour, amazed at my good fortune.

It was exhausting.

And then it was time to head to the meditation hall for the evening sit. I could barely keep my butt on my cushion and felt like I was bouncing up to the ceiling, and of course my focus, concentration and sense of calm were completely out of reach.

It was the longest and most uncomfortable hour of that retreat. And though I usually sleep well and deeply and instantly on retreat, not that night. I lay awake, buzzing, tossing and turning with all the excited thoughts and images and emotions coursing through my mind and body.

Completely exhausting.

It was like positivity on steroids. And I'd experienced highs like this many times for various reasons, but because I was so deep within the meditation and my awareness of sensations (it was already five days into the retreat), I was acutely in touch with all the nuances of what I was experiencing, moment by moment.

Highs / Lows

It was too much. And it was painful.

I thought I'd lived for the highs, strived for that 'bliss,' that ecstasy, those moments of "I did it!" or "I got it!" or "I *am* great!" That those were the ultimate goals, those extreme feelings of success and attainment of ideals.

Yes... and no.

The addict craves sensation, yet our beings thrive in calm and equanimity. Those extremes of emotion and sensation are very trying on our equilibrium, and even when it's a high and a positive situation, our system goes into overload trying to balance the extreme reactions, hence the craving for a drug or substance to level us out, and numb the intensity.

I'd always thought I craved the alcohol or drugs to celebrate my triumphs, while it was actually my being and body needing to level out and return to some sort of equilibrium and equanimity and diffuse the strain on my system.

Society and the media program us otherwise. Rather than promoting calm and contentment, we are pushed and triggered towards the opposite, all the time. Our fears are constantly being triggered, our instincts exploited to satisfy our every craving and whim, our anxieties fed with messages of needing more and more of whatever it is we are told we are lacking.

It is only in retreating from this onslaught of distraction and going into my own silence that I have been able to know what is important for me, what I truly need. It is in my silence that I have become aware of the similar effects of both extremes—the highs and the lows—and how both are equally detrimental to my balance and true happiness.

It's a profound revelation.

Our dragons we feed can be so deceptive. Who would have thought that the ego buzz from a positive achievement and the accolades forthcoming could be as psychologically unhealthy as a depressive low?

This is not to say we should not strive to achieve and reach our goals. What I have found is that our *reaction* is what is crucial. Our reaction is what creates our psychic 'ruts' and compulsive patterns.

It is in learning to accept all of our situations in a calm and balanced manner that we can achieve inner peace. The good, the bad, the highs, the lows—they are all parts of our story, and we are the ones who choose to add the drama that takes them to a different level, to an extreme feeling that reinforces previous patterns and behaviours.

We are the ones who pass judgement and add emotive reaction.

As we learn to let go of judgement and become an observer of our situations and stories, we let go, little by little, of our tenacious hold on these familiar ways of thinking.

It's not easy. Those dragons are unrelenting and unscrupulous in their determination to thrive and survive. But little by little, baby step by baby step, we can release our hold and set them—and ourselves—free.

Reflection

Position yourself comfortably in your quiet space. If writing appeals to you, have pen and paper ready, or better yet, a journal.

Close your eyes, and simply focus on your breath. Be aware of breathing in, breathing out, breathing in, breathing out, breathing in, breathing out.

Highs / Lows

The following questions or statements may be an aid to direct your inner work:

Think back to past high and low periods or situations in your life. How did you address and respond to these?

Think about the calm, relatively uneventful (not to be confused with bored) times in your life. Were your behaviours and reactions similar to the extreme times?

How does your body respond to both types of situations (extreme and uneventful)?

What types of activities do you tend to engage in within these two different modes?

ten

We must see all scars as beauty. Okay? This will be our secret. Because take it from me, a scar does not form on the dying. A scar means, 'I survived.'

– Chris Cleave,
Little Bee

Our Scars Mean We Have Survived

I spent most of my life loathing parts of myself, wanting to end them, get rid of them, cut them out of my life. That did not only include detrimental behaviours and compulsions, but also physical aspects of myself. As a teen, I hated my hair and for nearly all my adult life, I hated my acne and so I didn't like my face. And when eating became another compulsive behaviour I hated my extra weight. It took me a long time to accept all my behaviours, thought patterns, and attributes to realize that I am ALWAYS my truth (wise words from my old soul daughter at age twenty-three).

I always felt so much less than others, and so much less than my POTENTIAL.

I spent so much time comparing myself to others, or to an imaginary 'perfect me' that I could never attain, and this again led to my ego's obsession with self-abasement.

This seems to be particularly common in Western cultures. In a blog on addiction written by Allan Schwartz, Sharon Salzberg, one of the great teachers in Buddhist philosophy and mindful living, shares her experience while attending a conference years ago with the Dalai Lama:

> "What do you think about self-hatred?" I asked when it was my turn to bring up an issue for discussion. I was eager to get directly to the suffering I had seen so often in my students, a suffering I was familiar with myself. The room went quiet as all of us awaited the answer of the Dalai Lama, revered leader of Tibetan Buddhism. Looking startled, he turned to his translator and asked pointedly in Tibetan again and again for an explanation. Finally, turning back to me, the Dalai Lama tilted his head, his eyes narrowed in confusion. "Self-hatred?" he repeated in English. "What is that?"
>
> All of us gathered at that 1990 conference, India-philosophers, psychologists, scientists, and meditators were from Western countries, and self-hatred was something we immediately understood. (Schwartz)

Why is self-hate such a familiar concept in the Western world?

Maybe it's because we are always competing to be the best. It's not enough to be a responsible citizen and have a respectable career or trade unless you are the best in your field or making the most money possible. The further we are from our vision of perfection, the greater our self-hate can be.

Within this same blog, Allan Schwartz goes on to explain the connection between self-hate and addiction:

> In other words, the self-hate originates with the inevitable failure to be perfect. The greater the gap between what we wish

for and what we have, the greater the self-hate. This results in flagellating ourselves by submitting ourselves to endless criticism. Then, we attempt to hide the painful emotions behind this by drinking and taking drugs to numb the pain. What is tragic about this is that we are convinced, at least we in the West, that it is never acceptable to be average. No one stops to think about the fact that being average is a good thing. It is a good thing because what is most important is to embrace who we are. (Schwartz)

Why do we torture ourselves with expectations of how we should be, could be, would be if only we weren't so weak, or lazy, or unmotivated, or undisciplined, or stupid, or something else--the list is endless. We don't need others berating us. We are masters in the art. Why not live in the now, in and with our present reality, as it is? Why not embrace all our present ways of being and thinking and acting and reacting as the best we can be and do at this moment?

If you are reading this book, you have good intentions to keep growing within yourself. Wonderful! Most of us sincerely wish to do well within ourselves and towards others.

The behaviours we have created, and their subsequent consequences or physical ramifications are our personal barometer of our present state.

Embrace them. They are your story. YOUR story—the one you continue to create. And the act of creating is continuous and always changing, never the same from one moment to the next.

There is your freedom. You can create the next behaviour, you can change the present reaction, you can learn and modify and grow. So can your body, and so can your mind.

What is relevant is that I have learned to embrace my scars, my wrinkles, my weight—what society might call my 'imperfections.'

They are my story, my battle wounds, my struggles, and most importantly, they showcase my triumphant survival to this present moment. I wear them proudly. They are me, and I embrace them in gratitude. They are the reflections of a life lived, and they are my perfections, because they reflect the perfect me in this moment.

And now as I enter this new chapter of being an elder, I watch this body, which has carried me through all my various manifestations and behaviours and actions and reactions, present more and more aspects of aging. I see the same progression when I look at my friends, yet there is also a sense of magic, and a secret we all share as we age—we do not age within, unless we choose to. And that is a truth. I look at my friends with whom I have shared life since the age of eighteen, and I see them, still, at that age, or maybe slightly older, say twenty-five—a full-grown adult. I see their spirit in their eyes and their lively life essence in their loving smiles and their delicious laughs and their familiar gestures, and I see their 'scars' and 'battle wounds' and these are familiar also as part of their stories.

I feel that I've joined a secret society, and the secret is that age IS just a number. Yes, these miraculous 'meatsuits' are running down and getting tired, yet our essence within is still sharp and witty and oh-so-alive and oh-so-loving and so much richer and fuller in the wisdom we have attained.

So again, I embrace the aging process and I watch as this wonderful body changes and begins its decline, and attains more scars and carbuncles and battle wounds, and I am so very grateful to have made it to sixty, to this point, because some don't get that opportunity. I also recognize that the reality is from this point on it's basically a crap shoot, and we have no idea what the next moment holds.

But then, we never do, do we?

Change is the only constant. And that, for many of us, is the most frightening and unnerving truth. Because it can be incredibly painful, and it can be unbelievably difficult. But it can *be*, which means there is freedom for all of us should we choose it.

Why not live every moment to its fullest, and embrace where you are even if it feels like it may not be the 'optimum' choice possible?

Who's judging? Only you.

Accept yourself, accept your scars and 'imperfections,' accept your body as your story to the world. It is perfect in its reflection.

Reflection

Position yourself comfortably in your quiet space. If writing appeals to you, have pen and paper ready, or better yet, a journal.

Close your eyes, and simply focus on your breath. Be aware of breathing in, breathing out, breathing in, breathing out, breathing in, breathing out.

The following questions or statements may be an aid to direct your inner work:

What are the things you really don't like about yourself, inside or out?

Are these independent feelings, or based on comparison to others?

Are they able to be changed, or worthy of being changed—do they really matter?

Would you truly be a stronger, better person if they were changed?

Do you really want to change them?

How can you make this happen?

Sacred Path Card #13
Coral

If Coral has appeared in your cards today, you are being asked to look at the idea of nurturing. It may be time to nurture yourself or another. If you refuse to be nurtured it may be time to drop that superhuman attitude before you get sick. Coral tells us that our bodies have needs too. Pay attention and be good to your body.

Coral also speaks of the Planetary Family. If you feel lonely or alone, it may be time to have a reunion with the other creatures that share the Earth with you. Listen to All Our Relations and cut the "I'm the only one" refrain out of your thoughts.

Coral always tells us to listen to our feelings. If you have been ignoring how you feel around certain people or how your body feels, Coral is insisting that you reconnect to those feelings. Remember, to feel is to heal.
(Sams 122 -123)

eleven

In the process of letting go, you will lose many things from the past, but you will find yourself.

– Deepak Chopra

Letting Go

It sounds so simple, so freeing—"Let go!"

An image of releasing a balloon that floats gently up, up, up, until it's out of sight. An effortless opening of the hand, a softening of the clenched fist, an unfurling of the compressed fingers. . .

Such a lovely, freeing feeling; wouldn't that be something we'd all want and choose?

Not so much.

As simple as it sounds, as wonderful as it feels, as freeing as it is, letting go is one of the most difficult things to do.

To let go of our compulsive patterns, our familiar feelings, our set routines, our known habitats, our comforting habits, our safe, non-challenging relationships that allow us to remain in the status quo is SO HARD.

A wonderful and very wise friend told me this gem in regard to letting go of situations, or people, or places because sometimes we know we have to physically move on in our own growth and leave behind what is known and loved:

Letting go is like immigration.

You know in your heart that you have to leave the place of your birth or your family, because if not, you will not be able to be who you are meant to be, or you will not be able to offer your future generations more than what is available to you at present. You can stay, and maybe you'll be okay—you'll probably be somewhat safe, or at least, comforted in the familiar arms of what you know—but you'll be giving up the opportunity to possibly soar, and flourish and discover, and grow to heights not even visible to you from your present vantage point. And even though it will most likely be a painful struggle to make the change, you will be offering that same opportunity of a brighter future to your children or those that come after you or look up to you.

My father immigrated to Canada after World War II, at about the age of twenty-two. His mother had died when he was only three, and as an only child he was taken from his father at age seventeen to the work camps in Germany, and subsequently he served in the Polish army. During the war much of his home region was devastated and war-torn, and he had no idea if his father was still alive. When the war ended, he and the other veterans were given the opportunity to immigrate to either Australia or Canada, and my father chose Canada.

Imagine arriving in a foreign country, not knowing the language, having no contacts and very few possessions. This is the story of so many of our ancestors, and it may be your story. This is the ultimate letting go—letting go of everything because either there's nothing left for you where you are or you know that there's the possibility of a better outcome out there.

But it's so very scary. You're choosing to step into the unknown.

And it hurts to leave those loved ones and cherished places. Sometimes those loved ones don't want you to go, because you're leaving them behind and they're content enough in this same place and don't feel the same urge or desire—or courage—to leave everything for the possibility of something more, something better. They want you to stay with them and keep everything as it is.

Your journey may not be this drastic on a physical level, but the decision to let go of a lifestyle practice can be deeper and more difficult, because the opportunity to 'go back' is always there in front of you. Daily, hourly, sometimes moment by moment, you are making the choice to keep moving forward in your new life. Those memories of how it was can be sweetly deceptive and are always lurking in the background, waiting for a trigger to release their temptations of false comfort.

But nothing stays as it is; everything changes all the time. So trying to hold onto the myth of what was will only cause more suffering.

Yes, as the Buddha says, life is suffering. We get to choose which flavours of suffering we embrace and how we choose to live within it and react to it.

The pain of letting go of what we know is excruciating and scary, and those first steps on the journey are challenging and arduous, yet in time they can lead to discovering and exploring those heights and adventures and experiences that you know await you, that you feel in your core being are where you are supposed to go, where you *have* to go.

So you leave your 'country' and your loved ones behind to make a better life for you and your future generations, your legacy.

You begin the hero's journey. And you don't get to be called a hero by taking the easy road.

This journey most often is not a physical one. The steps needed to detach ourselves from our continuous drama, our replay of past events and regrets, our obsession with the 'what ifs' of the future—these can be as painful and heroic as the decision to cross the world and start a new life in a new land.

When our mind latches on to those old spirals and starts walking those familiar paths, it really does not want to get off, even though most of the time those familiar 'trips' are causing pain and suffering.

There can even be a sense of shirking responsibility in the thought of detaching: "If I stop thinking about it, something bad could happen!" As if your ruminations and dredging up of bad feelings or memories or failings can cause a positive change for someone else, or for you.

And this is not to say that processing or reflection or pondering is not helpful. Of course it is, and we all need more of that in our lives as opposed to the constant distraction of our screens and technology. It's the replay, replay, replay of familiar regrets or guilt of past choices and the snowballing effect of our fears that can be so damaging and immobilizing.

That's when we need to bring ourselves back to our present moment.

What is the reality RIGHT NOW?

Are you breathing?

Sometimes it needs to be as basic as that: Bring yourself back to your breath, breathing in, breathing out, breathing in, breathing out.

Open your eyes and look around you at your present state. If the walls are still standing and the roof is not threatening to crash down on you, breathe again, and be in your present moment.

That's all. No more.

Let go of those regrets and fears; unclench each one of those unrelenting knuckles that grips your being, that replays a regret, that feeds a dragon of fear, and allow your body to breathe and soften.

Let go.

Reflection

Position yourself comfortably in your quiet space. If writing appeals to you, have pen and paper ready, or better yet, a journal.

Close your eyes, and simply focus on your breath. Be aware of breathing in, breathing out, breathing in, breathing out, breathing in, breathing out.

The following questions or statements may be an aid to direct your inner work:

Think of a belief that causes you suffering. Is this belief true? Why do you think it is true?

Who would you be if you were able to let go of this belief?

What do you need to do to be able to let go of this belief?

twelve

If your compassion does not include yourself, it is incomplete.

– Jack Kornfield,
Buddha's Little Instruction Book

Self-love, self-respect, self-worth: There's a reason they all start with 'self.' You can't find them in anyone else.

– Unknown

Compassion and Loving Kindness

Most of us would consider ourselves compassionate people. We genuinely feel for and care for others, and generally do not wish harm or ill-will towards others. In most areas of our society, our values are modelled and directed towards treating others as we would like to be treated, and of course there are variations of the 'Golden Rule' within just about every belief system:

Do unto others as you would have done to you.

It's a good thing that this maxim does not imply "Do unto others as you do unto yourself" because many of us would probably end up in correctional institutions or at the very least completely isolated and without relationships on any level.

It's fairly easy and it comes fairly naturally to treat others civilly and with kindness, but how often does that same respect and tolerant consideration apply to ourselves?

Listen—really listen—to the way you speak to yourself. You may be appalled, and chances are you're already aware of it. If you are reading this book, there's a good chance you've done your share of self-abasement, shaming, or torture. We would never address another person in the way we often castigate ourselves. Yet we continue to do so, especially if we are struggling with a compulsive/repulsive behaviour; each time we 'fail' and fall short of our self-set standards is another opportunity for an internal flogging.

And if we're really a pro at self-condemnation, we react in this way to situations out of our control.

I was the victim of a rape in my mid-twenties. As I found out after the fact, the perpetrator had been stalking me and knew where I lived, and attacked me as I entered my home after a late-night shift at the restaurant. At that time I was renting an upstairs apartment in a home outside the city, so when I initially screamed for help, no one heard me. And when he responded by jabbing me in the middle of my back, saying he had a gun and would kill me if I continued to scream, obviously I complied and, feeling that I was completely on my own to survive this, continued to be compliant as he forced me into my apartment.

There's no need to go into the details of what transpired over the next two or three hours; I was tied up and violated in my home. Besides being the victim of rape which is devastating within itself, I also had to deal with having the sanctuary of my home stolen from me. And perhaps even more difficult is knowing later that he most likely did not have a weapon—could I have defended myself and stopped him rather than falling into the Stockholm Syndrome and 'befriending' him so that he wouldn't kill me?

Through our interactions, I discovered that he knew me, though he wore a balaclava the entire time, so I wasn't able to recognize him. I was so traumatized that I could barely remember any details when first questioned by police, and in their efforts to proceed, I was taken to a hypnotist in order to relive the violation to hopefully recall details for their investigation. Imagine how much I wanted to do that. . . But it helped, though there was not enough evidence to lay charges on the perpetrator unfortunately.

There were two important pieces for me in my recovery process. One was to somehow feel safe again within my home. I never stayed in that apartment again, and was fortunate that one of my brothers offered me a place in his home until I could find something else. And though I did get an apartment shortly after with a friend (as I was too frightened to live on my own), a couple months later I decided to pack up my car and drive solo across the country to Vancouver, British Columbia, because I did not want to live having to look over my shoulder in fear every moment. Truth be told, there are still moments where I'm triggered when I'm walking alone in isolated places. I've come to accept that and know that they quickly pass.

The biggest piece, though, was in forgiving myself: "Why me? What did I do to deserve this? There's a reason why this happened to me. Did I cause this, bring this about somehow through my own actions? Why didn't I try to stop it?"

I know I'm not alone in these feelings. It's common for victims to blame ourselves, especially if our self-worth is already non-existent. I'll never know why this happened to me, but I do know that I acted in my best interests for survival, and I have accepted that and am very grateful that more harm—internal or external—was not inflicted. Through counselling with Victim Services and after many years of letting go of my guilt and self-judgement, bit by bit, I've come to a place of peace within this particular life experience.

There are other areas, most prominently in my addictive behaviours, where the process continues.

According to Dr. Kristin Neff, author of the great resource *Self-Compassion*, much of our lack of self-compassion comes from both a constant comparison with others and an unfounded need for perfection:

> Continually feeding our need for positive self-evaluation is a bit like stuffing ourselves with candy. We get a brief sugar high, then a crash . . .and a pendulum swing to despair. . . We can't always feel special and above average. . . So what's the answer? To stop judging and evaluating ourselves altogether. To stop trying to label ourselves as 'good' or 'bad' and simply accept ourselves with an open heart. To treat ourselves with the same kindness, caring, and compassion we would show to a good friend, or even a stranger for that matter. (Neff 5 - 6)

I can hear your rebuttal: "Yeah, but that's about *normal* people, or at least people who aren't as messed up as me with my addiction to alcohol/drug/food/sex/gambling/shopping etc. etc. I am really fucked up."

And there it is.

I'm not discounting that you may have a serious issue that has negatively affected your family life, friendships, jobs, financial security, etc. But the self-talk has the same effect on all of us, no matter what we are battling. Learning to have compassion for yourself is a huge step towards the way out of the mire, whereas making yourself feel worse through your own shaming often brings you back to the substance or behaviour that, for a brief moment, makes you feel better, until you crash again.

As long as we are loathing those behaviours and condemning ourselves in the process, we will continue that awful cycle. It is a really scary and chaotic world out there, and many of us have never had solid trustworthy and respected role models to help us navigate through it. No wonder we opted for ways to manage. There are all kinds of quick-fix options constantly bombarding us through the media and by our peers; it takes a strong individual with healthy support systems to steer clear of all the crutches.

Be gentle with yourself. Talk to yourself as you would to your child, or your dearest friend, or your loving pet even. Understand that you are doing your best. Very few of us wish intentional harm on ourselves or on others. Yes, at times of fits of rage or depths of despair we can make devastating choices, yet those are born of our fears and our pain and our suffering. Acknowledge that you are hurting, accept that you are really struggling. Be kind and tender in your self-talk. And, as Kristin Neff suggests, give yourself a hug:

> Hugging Practice – One easy way to soothe and comfort yourself when you're feeling badly is to give yourself a gentle hug. It seems a bit silly at first, but your body doesn't know that. It just responds to the physical gesture of warmth and care, just as a baby responds to being held in its mother's arms. Our skin is an incredibly sensitive organ. Research indicates that physical touch releases oxytocin, provides a sense of security, soothes distressing emotions and calms cardiovascular stress. So why not try it? If you notice that you're feeling tense, upset, sad, or self-critical, try giving yourself a warm hug, tenderly stroking your arm or face, or gently rocking your body. What's important is that you make a clear gesture that conveys feelings of love, care, and tenderness. . . Notice how your body feels after receiving the hug. It's amazing how easy it is to tap into the oxytocin system and change your biochemical experience. Try giving yourself a hug in times of suffering several

times a day for a period of at least a week. Hopefully you'll start to develop the habit of physically comforting yourself when needed, taking full advantage of this surprisingly simple and straightforward way to be kind to ourselves. (Neff 49 -50)

Once you open and soften your heart to your own pain, you can begin to find ways to help yourself. Perhaps you can reach out to a professional counselor who is trained to walk others through their fears and triggers to begin unravelling those well-tied knots. Maybe there is a friend or loved one you trust, with whom you can begin the conversation of self-forgiveness.

No one method is correct, and no method is a fool-proof healer for everyone.

Begin by softening to yourself, acknowledging and honouring your struggle. It is not something to be hated and ripped out of your life. Embrace wherever you are at this moment and begin there.

Be gentle and kind with yourself. You deserve mercy.

Reflection

Position yourself comfortably in your quiet space. If writing appeals to you, have pen and paper ready, or better yet, a journal.

Close your eyes, and simply focus on your breath. Be aware of breathing in, breathing out, breathing in, breathing out, breathing in, breathing out.

The following questions or statements may be an aid to direct your inner work:

Compassion and Loving Kindness

What are the situations you most regret, those where you have struggled the most in forgiving yourself?

If someone you loved had committed these same acts, how would you find it in your heart to forgive them?

Pretend you are someone who truly loves you and explain why and how you forgive you.

Practice self-hugging, including the gentle nurturing comments you need to hear.

thirteen

Every one of us is losing something precious to us. Lost opportunities, lost possibilities, feelings we can never get back again. That's part of what it means to be alive.

— Haruki Murakami, *Kafka on the Shore*

What we have once enjoyed and deeply loved we can never lose, for all that we love deeply becomes a part of us.

— Helen Keller

The Grieving

Loss.

It's part of life. We are always losing opportunities or people or relationships or jobs or homes, pieces of ourselves that we need to learn to live without. Grief has many different shades and depths.

Sometimes we lose our dreams. My mid-twenties felt like all my dreams were being ripped away from me.

After the unresolved court case for the rape and the solo road trip across Canada, I settled in Vancouver and started to create a new life for myself, hoping to be physically far away from the fears that resided in my hometown and the compulsion to look over my shoulder in fear of pursuit and attack. It was at my serving job that I met the next piece of my journey—a young male regular with whom I fell madly and immediately in 'love.' We spent the next couple of months together and I believed I'd found The One in this humble, unpretentious cowboy from Alberta. At that time, I'd decided to go back to school and was saving to attend university that fall. Before meeting him, I'd already made plans to head up to Dawson City in the Yukon territory, where apparently one could make good money during the tourist season from May to August. He was needing a place to live at that time, so I let him stay in my apartment during those months, and we made plans that he would come to visit when possible.

We kept in touch as much as possible in that time of no internet and expensive long distance phone calls, and he did come to see me at one point. He'd told me that he'd paid off my credit card balance and offered to take my savings back with him to deposit in Vancouver where "it would be safer than a small bank in the Yukon." How dumb can a girl be. . .

A couple weeks after he left, I received a note in the mail from a close friend in Vancouver, who warned me that this love of my life "was not who he appeared to be." Turns out he was sleeping with another friend of mine, and when I returned home shortly after, fearing the worst, he was nowhere to be found, my savings were gone, my credit card balance was unpaid and I discovered that I was only one of a number of women who'd suffered similar treatment in his history.

Emotionally betrayed, financially violated, trust depleted and dreams destroyed.

Loss.

Yes, this was a very tangible loss, and it was obvious to all that there would be a valid and justifiable grieving process following it.

The Grieving

But there are other life events that may not be as evident in invoking grief. Choosing to let go of any deep-rooted habitual behaviour patterns can generate a void and an emptiness where there once was comfort and reprieve—a huge loss.

Let's face it—that's what this change means. You are choosing to let go of a coping mechanism that has been a part of your life for a very long time.

In the beginning, it represents a HUGE deprivation, a monumental void in your known lifestyle and approach to your day-to-day, your interactions, your socializing, your relationships, pretty much everything. There's no sugar-coating it. And there's no avoiding it.

Sorry.

I remember thinking that I wouldn't be able to attend any social engagements at first, that it would be far too awkward and uncomfortable without a drink in my hand. I remember feeling like I'd never be able to really have fun and let loose again. I remember questioning whether I'd have to change my whole social life. And it all made me so sad.

I remember feeling like I'd never be able to get through those difficult moments of stress, or anxiety or grief or even boredom without some kind of substance to ease my pain and take me to an easier state of mind.

And another loss that merits acknowledgement is the loss of all of those well-rehearsed rituals that accompany your habit. This actually became clearer to me in a dream after more than a year being intoxicant-free.

In the dream I was prepping my next high, thinking about where I was picking up the weed and from whom, and I was really pumped because I hadn't been high for a while. The anticipation and the visualization and expectations of that first luscious buzz were achingly tangible. I could taste it, I could smell it and I could not wait to have it... and then the deal fell through.

Crushed, thoroughly pissed, frantic—the craving was off the charts, and I immediately went into plan B mode. Okay, who else? Where else? I want it, I need it, I gotta get it.

And then I woke up. First thought was, oh my god, did I really smoke? And then the absolute relief that it was 'only a dream.'

I use quotation marks there because it was so real. It was unnerving that the pattern of thinking was so familiar, the steps so established, so easily triggered and re-enacted. It all felt no less a part of me than one of my limbs, for god's sake.

But it clearly showed me the pattern, the ritual, the dance. And those rituals and behaviours often take up a significant portion of our day. What kind of alcohol/drug will I get? Do I have enough at home already? Where and when will I get it? Do I need to juggle funds to make the purchase? How long will the supply last? Will I have enough? Where am I going to consume it? Is it an alone binge or a party with friends? Will I have enough? How high/drunk can I get—what's on tomorrow's agenda, and does it matter anyway? Will I have enough? Do I have my favorite supply of munchies? Have I covered every possible craving? WILL THERE BE ENOUGH?

It's an inner replay of a very familiar story, and we have mastered the lines, the comebacks, the acts to follow.

And then, in making this other choice, all of that is gone. You can rationalize that you're better off without this frenetic routine, but it doesn't make that initial void any less desolate.

That's why choosing to make this change and walk this new path takes so much courage. It's really difficult to choose to be present, every day, every moment, to every changing emotion and circumstance, to every initial overwhelming feeling of loss.

But know that you CAN. You can learn to ride the waves, to surf the tsunamis of chaos, and soar through the skies of elation without needing some substance as your leveller or your crutch.

And in those moments of immobilizing loss, know that if you can allow the pain its voice and expression, those moments will not last. They are not immortal, but only feel that way when we choose to accept them as integral parts of our being and we keep them trapped and suppressed and guarded by that dragon that tells us we can't handle it: "Don't go there, don't think about it, push it down, WAY down, and do something—ANYTHING—to take your mind off it."

And so, in that way, we actually give that pain and grief more power, and we feed that dragon's beliefs and make that loss more painful.

Grief is often associated with the loss of a loved one, but it can also be debilitating in the loss of a situation, a past-time, a tradition, a ritual, a career, or, in this case, a comforting coping strategy, that familiar friend I could cuddle up with for that loving numbing comfort.

I've spoken at length in previous chapters about the sense of deprivation and injustice that is very often experienced in making this change, and the deep grief from our sense of loss needs to be addressed as well.

Grieving is rarely a speedy process; when we least expect it, it can rush upon us in suffocating and unprecedented waves, and it is in these times, caught off guard, that it is most difficult to maintain our ground and the progress we've made.

It can be disguised as one of our 'triggers,' and just as a trigger unleashes an instantaneous mechanism, the wall around our well of grief and pain can be impulsively sprung with a flood of past or present hurts and we are overcome with the need to STOP it immediately, at all costs. There's no thought of "Wait, what are my tools at times like these?" We just need it to stop. And these are the times when we sometimes cave.

Understand that there will be many, many very challenging moments and situations ahead. But also know that each time you choose to stay your ground and not veer so easily into that familiar rut and succumb to the numbing substance or behaviour, each time you are rewiring that mechanism so that it will get set off less and less, and will continue to lose its power as you feed and nurture and strengthen your new coping strategies and allow that trigger to run through you and out of you.

And each time you are lighter.

There is a palpable release and a weight that is lifted, not to any extent of euphoria—at least not in that moment—but there is a calm, a quiet within, usually with tinges of sadness. But the overwhelming and immobilizing weight of grief has been lifted. Another face of it may return at a later date, but something has been liberated.

That being said, I don't believe we ever fully lose anything that we experience. Just as our bodies bear our life markings and scars, our soul, our spirit, our psychological being carries bits of all aspects of our existence. And in that case, we never completely lose anything that was once a part of us. It's like losing a loved one, yet feeling them always remaining within our hearts and our memories. As time passes, the intense grief subsides and you learn to live your life in a different way without their physical presence. You come to a point where you can hold those past experiences close to your heart and remember what once was and what helped you in your journey to where you are now, without craving it—whether it is a person, a substance, or a circumstance.

Life is always changing, whether we like it or not. Hopefully, most of us are moving towards more positive change, and believe me, if you continue on this path, there are positive rewards within the changes. You will have new experiences that are fun, and fuller and richer because you are present and your reality is not tainted by distorting substances or mired in remorse and regret for impulsive or undesirable actions. You will become more empowered, happier within yourself, more easily able to meet your eyes in the mirror with love and acceptance.

Our struggles, our losses, our comforts, our loves, our highs, our lows—they all leave their imprint on and in our being. We absorb them into whatever it is that we are truly made of and they shape our passage, our behaviours, our relationships, our stories.

Let go of those heavy restraining pieces that are causing you suffering. Acknowledge their impact and value in your personal growth, and understand that it is okay now to let the weight of them go, accepting the gifts of change they have brought you.

It is much easier to walk to the summit with less to carry.

Reflection

Position yourself comfortably in your quiet space. If writing appeals to you, have pen and paper ready, or better yet, a journal.

Close your eyes, and simply focus on your breath. Be aware of breathing in, breathing out, breathing in, breathing out, breathing in, breathing out.

The following questions or statements may be an aid to direct your inner work:

Think of some of the deep losses in your life.

Where do you feel the loss in your body? Can you describe what it feels like?

Are there particular activities or encounters that tend to bring this sensation of loss to the forefront for you? Can you think of any response or reaction that could ease these times for you—a chat with a friend, getting out for a walk in nature, journaling?

As you reflect on this loss, can you find at least one bit of light and positivity that was given to you in relation to it—one thing you may have learned, one thing that may have made you stronger, improved future relationships, or grew your heart?

fourteen

It is in transparency that we open to blossom and flourish and grow strong.

— Dianne Szymanski Krynicki

Don't Give Away Your Power

There were many laws of nature (they called them Universal Laws) shared in that first meditation group I joined at the age of eighteen. These same laws or truths continued and still continue to show up in my life, and I know them to be ultimately true. Concepts like: Thoughts are Things (all thoughts manifest into some sort of energy), Change is the only Constant, What you put out will come back to you. Then there's this one: There is no such thing as a Secret.

Scary, huh?

What about all those horrible or revealing things we all try so desperately to hide?

Unfortunately, the manner in which this particular concept was presented to us was during one of the advanced courses of this meditation practice, and through what was essentially a brain-washing technique often used by cults.

Participants would first complete a four-day course (Inward Bound Four) which was based on teaching a simple meditation technique, included a memory-stimulating exercise, and ended with a loving and healing energy exchange for all of mankind. At the end of this we were all ready to embrace and love the world, and eager to recruit new members. Then if you wanted to go further, there was a residential seven-day program (Inward Bound Seven) which promised even deeper insight and revelations. Of course I eagerly signed up, against my parents' wishes (as it cost $1,000 and I had to borrow the money), but hey, I was eighteen and an 'adult.'

Only twenty-four participants could enroll in each session. We arrived at our resort in Niagara-on-the-Lake (it was at a different location each time) and I anticipated an enlightening, love-filled, educational experience with this group in whom I'd placed complete trust.

And yeah...not so much...

Upon entering the conference room that first evening, it was very evident that this was an entirely different ball game. They had simulated an arena setting by creating a semi-circle of tables and chairs, and we were greeted with stern and solemn gazes from the organizers and aides as we entered the room. No shades of love, peace and happiness anywhere in the room.

They proceeded to grant each of us an 'arena.' When it was your turn, you were brought to the middle of this conclave and basically stripped of any psychological preservation you may have had.

In preparation, the organizers would have sought out all they could about you: any hidden humiliations, homosexual latency, relationships gone wrong, dysfunctional upbringing—anything they could use to 'reveal' you and basically break you down. 'Breaking you down' would generally mean having you collapse in tears with acknowledgement of your baseness. And if they couldn't break you verbally, they would often throw jugs of ice-cold water on those who were stoic in their denial, trying to make you lose control emotionally and psychologically.

After their 'success'—when you were emotionally crushed, humiliated and stripped of all human dignity—they would praise you for your honesty and openness and hug you with promises of unconditional love from all members present from that moment on. Now you could start again, fresh and free from those debilitating encumberments, ready to rebuild a stronger, better and more open you—with all of their help, of course.

This was their premise to prove that there was no such thing as a secret, because all could be and was revealed.

And it was done with the belief of making you stronger, more authentic, freer.

There is no question that this was a completely unacceptable practice, and it was a terrifying and humiliating exercise that I don't condone in any way.

And yet, I did gain some insight within my subsequent processing.

Through this experience, I learned at the young age of eighteen that we have all done and said and thought similar 'bad' things—being human means we may not always make the best of choices, we may hurt ourselves and others in the process, we may regret some actions and then try to hide them, or repress them, and definitely *not* share them with others. Heaven forbid! But there is a real and true empowerment in the idea of there being no secrets.

Anyone who has struggled with addictive behaviours and substance abuse has multitudes and layers upon layers of situations they want to keep hidden, shame that they bury deep within. Many of us spend much of our lives creating personas we present to the world, being very careful in all we say and do and how we look in order to maintain the façade. And in present times, we can multiply that tenfold with social media.

It takes *so* much energy to maintain the guise, always being careful to defend your position, prove your pretense and not slip up. It can be exhausting and anxiety-provoking to say the least. And for what end? So that you can never feel free to be 'exposed,' to be truly open, and completely genuine?

Anyone who has attended an Alcoholics Anonymous (AA) meeting knows the absolute relief and liberation and lightness in finally being able to reveal some of your worst moments and deepest shame, your lowest indignities and most profound regrets, and still be accepted within the group. These are admitted by your choice, and when you are ready, and not to be compared with the stripping down of my previous example in the 'arena.'

Many people in AA have come to a place of much calmer peace by admitting faults and transgressions and making amends. This same peace can be found at times within counselling. If you are fortunate enough to be matched with a good professional with whom you resonate, great strides can be made in unloading your hidden and secret baggage.

There is a real and true empowerment within the commitment of being true with yourself, a clear and untainted strength in being able to look at yourself in the mirror, deep within your own eyes, and accept who you are, with all your stories and histories and joys and pains.

When you squander your power and energy in constantly building and sustaining the persona you feel you need to present to the world, there is not as much left within for you to give to what truly makes you happy and fulfilled. You become unsure of who you really are and what it is that brings you joy.

If you have struggled with any kind of substance abuse, eating disorder or other compulsive behaviour, it is usually pretty clear who or what controls your power.

In the words of F. Scott Fitzgerald, "First you take a drink, then the drink takes a drink, then the drink takes you" (The Baltimore Literary Heritage Project).

And this is not only true in alcohol consumption. If you have suffered through any kind of binging behaviour—overeating, gambling, compulsive spending—you are very familiar with the spiral that most often occurs after the first cave-in.

With even the least bit of mindfulness, we know the moments, minutes, hours accumulating into days when either our minds or our physical bodies have been under the spell of our desired craving. When you suffer with addictive tendencies you are very familiar with giving away your power, often without a moment's hesitation. It's so easy and comforting and familiar to tread that well-worn and intimate path, that rut you've slipped into more often than not that you know so well and that feels so good.

. . .until you are completely powerless.

And completely absorbed in your self-loathing.

If you have ever made the choice—even for a short period—to abstain from your habitual and detrimental compulsion, you know the high of that other side. You've experienced the strength and purity of feeling authentic and true.

Imagine carrying that within you all the time. Imagine having basically nothing to hide, being able to look yourself and others clearly in the eye, never having to do a mental double-take to be sure you're giving the 'right' information, or sticking to the same story, or maintaining the persona you've previously honed and perfected.

Imagine the power in just being you.

Not being afraid to let people see who you really are. Not having to pretend to be someone you've imagined you should be. Not having to spend so much energy keeping it all together. Not creating all that unnecessary anxiety and stress within.

And then, not only having a sense of peace and acceptance and calm within, but feeling strong and so empowered to be true within yourself, and to have so much more energy to give in life, either in pursuing creative endeavours and personal aspirations or giving more genuine time and energy in your relationships.

It does sound idyllic. And it is possible. It's real, and it can be manifested in your life.

You can be your authentic and true self.

You're the one who gave away your power, and you're the one who can take it back.

Reflection

Position yourself comfortably in your quiet space. If writing appeals to you, have pen and paper ready, or better yet, a journal.

Close your eyes, and simply focus on your breath. Be aware of breathing in, breathing out, breathing in, breathing out, breathing in, breathing out.

The following questions or statements may be an aid to direct your inner work:

What is your biggest secret? Can you at the very least share it with yourself, and allow the slightest release in being able to look at it? Imagine, then, the relief in being able to let it go and not have to worry about being 'exposed.' Is there a way that this is possible?

What would it mean to live an open and honest life? List the positives as well as the difficulties.

fifteen

Acknowledging the good that you already have in your life is the foundation for all abundance.

— Eckhart Tolle,
A New Earth: Awakening to Your Life's Purpose

'Enough' is a feast.

— Buddhist proverb

Gratitude

A book that has made quite a stir in the last couple decades is *The Secret* by Rhonda Byrne. The basic concept described in the book is not only to be grateful for all that you already have, but to be grateful for all that you would like to have, as if you already have it. The more you shift your thought patterns into images and beliefs of abundance, the more abundance will be created in your life. It's that simple 'glass half empty/half full' concept, and brings us back to the realization that it's all a state of mind.

What is it that you are focusing on?

Though some may scoff at its simplicity and naïve message, it's true, and it works.

Developing a practice of gratitude has enriched my life beyond belief. It helped me to work through a difficult and unhappy marriage and create a new and different and richer and fuller life than I imagined.

As a life-long journaler, in my darkest and most difficult times, I began to include gratitude journaling in my daily morning writing. Each and every day I wrote pages of all that I was grateful for and all that I hoped to be grateful for in the future:

> *I am so very grateful. I am so very grateful for my sobriety, my clarity and energy, my wonderful daughters, my new supportive and loving relationship, my lovely light-filled home, my great job and financial security, my new vehicle, my lovely clear skin, great health and amazingly fit body, and all the wonderful people coming into my life to serve and learn from and grow with to create positive opportunities for us all.*

Not all of this was actually true at the time; I didn't have a new and loving relationship, or a new vehicle, or completely clear skin, or an amazingly fit body. But I was grateful for these things coming into my life every day, as much as I was grateful for all that I already had.

I continued this for a few years, until I came to a place where I realized it had all manifested. Granted, I was also doing a lot of inner work in mindfulness and my meditation practice. The morning gratitude journaling served a great purpose of setting my intention for the day and keeping in mind the type of life I wanted to be living. And it didn't matter that it was repetitive; in fact, I think it works to an advantage as you keep the same ideas in the forefront of your consciousness day after day, moment after moment, reinforcing them in the same way and making them a part of you. And it's okay to 'fake it till you make it' if it's not feeling right, as it often won't, depending on the day. But keeping these ideas in your conscious mind and physically writing them every day can have very positive effects regardless.

Gratitude

I continued this until I took the life shifting ten-day Vipassana course. At that point my gratitude practice had become such a part of me that it didn't feel necessary to keep repeating what I already had, as I was moving forward in other ways. But it wasn't long before I took it up again, realizing its importance in setting my intention at the beginning of every day, and in keeping in mind new goals and present moments for gratitude. It really is a wonderful way to start your day.

And yet, I was still struggling with my broken more-is-better marijuana switch. I would stop smoking for a month, two months, three months, and then would hit a trigger situation that would completely unbalance me and I would start smoking again, usually in moderation at first, and in no time, be right back into more-is-better.

It seemed like a lost cause, an incurable state of mind/body/habit.

Then I decided to try writing myself out of it. I had made huge changes in my life in other less pervasive and controlling issues—why not this?

So, here is what I started to add to my daily journaling:

> *I am so very grateful to be good with being straight, to no longer need or want pot to numb my pain or distort my reality, to be present with what is and know that my discomfort will pass, that nothing lasts forever.*

And then I took it all even further and started writing this book. And then my gratitude journaling included: "*I am so very grateful to now be writing and creating and channeling the book that will help me and help so many others.*"

And here it is, in your hands. This stuff works!

Recently I had a wonderful a-ha moment in retrospect of my childhood and realized I had been introduced to the power of gratitude at a much younger age. When I was twelve, my mother's employer passed on a set of books no longer being used by their family. These were the *Pollyanna* collection, also known as *The Glad Books*, written by Eleanor H. Porter, starting in 1912. The main character, Pollyanna, is an eleven-year-old girl who is orphaned when her father, her only surviving parent and a poor pastor of a missionary church, dies unexpectedly. She must go live with her maiden aunt, Polly, a stiff and bitter woman who begrudgingly takes her niece in strictly out of duty. In no time, Pollyanna transforms the household and the community with her 'glad game.' As she explains to Nancy, her aunt's kind servant, her father received only a meagre salary, and he and his daughter were dependent on help from the community in the form of missionary barrels, so he taught her the 'game':

> "'You don't seem ter see any trouble bein' glad about everythin',' retorted Nancy, choking a little over her remembrance of Pollyanna's brave attempts to like the bare little attic room.
>
> Pollyanna laughed softly.
>
> 'Well, that's the game, you know, anyway.'
>
> "The –game?"
>
> 'Yes; the 'just being glad' game. . . we began it on some crutches that came in a missionary barrel.'
>
> 'Crutches!'
>
> 'Yes. You see I'd wanted a doll, and father had written them so; but when the barrel came the lady wrote that there hadn't any dolls come in, but the little crutches had. So she sent 'em along as they might come in handy for some child, sometime. And that's when we began it.'
>
> 'Well, I must say I can't see any game about that, about that,' declared Nancy, almost irritably.

'Oh, yes; the game was to just find something about everything to be glad about—no matter what 'twas,' rejoined Pollyanna, earnestly. 'And we began right then—on those crutches.'

'Well, goodness me! I can't see anythin' ter be glad about—getting' a pair of crutches when you wanted a doll!'

'Why, just be glad because you *don't—need—'em!*' exulted Pollyanna, triumphantly. 'You see it's just as easy—when you know how!'" (Porter 42 – 44)

Pollyanna becomes the darling of the town, and when she loses the ability to walk due to an accident caused by a negligent driver, yet still finds reasons to be grateful and happy in life, she has everyone in her midst playing the 'glad game' and creating new and happier lives as a result.

We can all do this.

We can all make these changes that will bring us more happiness, we can all shift our thinking in order to create perspectives of have rather than have not, do rather than do not, can rather than cannot. We can thrive rather than degenerate. We can let go of those dragons that hide our reasons for gratitude from us and realize and reap the treasures of abundance within.

Reflection

Position yourself comfortably in your quiet space. If writing appeals to you, have pen and paper ready, or better yet, a journal.

Close your eyes, and simply focus on your breath. Be aware of breathing in, breathing out, breathing in, breathing out, breathing in, breathing out.

The following questions or statements may be an aid to direct your inner work:

Make a list of all the things you already have and reasons you're grateful. Begin each statement with: "I am grateful for…"

Now continue that same list with all the things, attributes, relationships, changes, etc. that you wish you had presently, and still begin each statement with "I am grateful for," writing in the present tense as though it is already part of your life.

Choose the most important ones and find time each day when you can actively acknowledge these and perhaps write them down, every day.

Sacred Path Card #40
Great Smoking Mirror

The Great Smoking Mirror reflects the lesson of leaving the myth behind. You are what you decide you are. Remove the smoke screen that hides your natural talents or worth, and stand tall. Recognize the areas to be developed further and begin that process. Stop cowering before your potential and live your truth. There are millions of role models to choose from.

On another level you are being asked to be a good reflection for others. Encourage others to be bold through Walking Your Talk. The reflections you see in others may not make you happy if you are doubting yourself and your right to be. Jealousy on any level only inhibits growth and wastes energy. Shatter the mirrors that insist on self-importance, gloom, or failure so you can get down to what's really important.

On all levels, the Smoking Mirror asks us to accept light and shadow as equal. The reflections we dislike can be worthy opponents who teach us to grow into our potential. Even our shadow sides serve us by leading us through trial and error to the true image of Self. (Sams 295 – 296)

sixteen

Drama does not just walk into our lives. Either we create it, invite it, or associate with it.

– Brandi L. Bates,
Remains To Be Seen

The Drama Dragon

We are our Story. We thrive on Story. Our Story of our self gives us our sense of who we are, what is important to us, what has shaped our thoughts, our relationships, our journey, our concept of self. Without our Story—which is made up of our past stories and relies on our future stories for its continued survival—we feel we have no self.

We all have memories of situations, events, conflicts, and relationships that shape our perspective of the world and of ourselves. That perspective is continuously fed and nurtured and molded with our thoughts and our beliefs about what is true. It all comes back to what we're feeding our thoughts. When we make the choice to become aware of the endless chatter of our minds, it's fascinating (and disconcerting) to start really listening to our stories.

When I started mindfulness meditation in my late forties, I couldn't believe the negativity and bitchiness of my inner conversations. It was no wonder I was so unhappy in so many areas of my life. In my mind I would go on and on about how awful this person was, or what a terrible thing that person had done to me, or how I was the one who always had to do everything and was never appreciated, and I would carry on full out conversations with those with whom I was in conflict, providing both sides of the story to fuel my justifications for their incompetence and malevolence and my victimization. As I became more and more aware of my inner voice, I don't know how often I would stop dead in my self-talk in a shock of revelation at the stories I was creating—and believing.

Our 'truths' are based on our experiences and the belief systems we create. This is perfectly illustrated in this well-known Native allegory:

Two Wolves – A Cherokee Legend

An old Cherokee is teaching his grandson about life. "A fight is going on inside of me," he said to the boy.

"It is a terrible fight and it is between two wolves. One is evil—he is anger, envy, sorrow, regret, greed, arrogance, self-pity, guilt, resentment, inferiority, lies, false pride, superiority, and ego."

He continued, "The other is good—he is joy, peace, love, hope, serenity, humility, kindness, benevolence, empathy, generosity, truth, compassion, and faith. The same fight is going on inside you—and inside every other person, too."

The grandson thought about it for a minute and then asked his grandfather, "Which wolf will win?"

The old Cherokee simply replied, "The one you feed."

(First People of America and Canada – Turtle Island)

As the allegory shows, one of the steps toward freedom from compulsive behaviours is to become aware of the thought patterns we are nurturing. And given that compulsive and addictive behaviours carry such a compelling, overpowering force within them, we are easily overcome in our innate intentions to 'be good.' More often than not, the compulsion succeeds, and we succumb to the flood of drama that fills our being: "How could I have done this again?!" "What is wrong with me?" "Why am I so fucked up?" and on and on. And because we often live big, and party big, and spend big or gamble big, our drama is HUGE.

Granted, we are all the centre of our own universe and most of us have a tendency to exaggerate whatever happens to us, but those of us with addictive behaviours tend to take it to a whole other level. We are award-winning actors within our self-produced tragedies.

We are feeding the thought pattern. It is gorging itself on the intense feast of our self-denegation and the pattern grows stronger and goes deeper.

What if you didn't believe you were an addict? What if you truly *knew* that that is not who you are? What if you didn't compound the relapse, the binge with the incessant barrage of you'll never learn, you'll never change, you'll never be 'good' or 'enough' or 'worthy'?

What if you turned off the drama?

We have created our beliefs about ourselves, and we are the only ones who can let them go.

If you are not familiar with *The Work* of Byron Katie, I strongly suggest you take a look at her website or one of her many self-help books. She offers life-changing suggestions and steps in releasing those deep-seated beliefs that are no longer serving us. Though the premise behind *The Work* is simple, the questions she challenges you to ask yourself about your convictions can create huge transitions in your life. I could summarize it here, but she deserves the credit for her insight, and if you are motivated to change, and for it to be effective for you, you need to take the steps to discover it for yourself.

On this journey to make a change within yourself, be assured that you may not be 100% successful all the time (and that, of course, is a *slight* understatement). I have been on the planet for six decades and five of them have been battling compulsive behaviours of some sort. Step by step, change by change, minor shift by minor shift, moment by moment, I am sometimes leaping, sometimes crawling, sometimes tiptoeing, sometimes resting on the sidelines, and often taking three steps back.

But overall, I am moving forward.

And I am learning that I need to stop feeding those immutable beliefs that keep me chained to thinking, "This is who I am."

So you have a relapse? So you're unable to quit cold turkey? So you have three months of sobriety and then you cave? It *isn't* all over. In those three months you have created tangible change within your wiring and yes, you may have gone deep down into your most familiar comforting binge, but you can move on from there.

And you are not starting from ground zero. You have not completely negated all those days and moments of behaving in ways more preferable for your health and well-being. You cannot eradicate them—you're not omnipotent.

Rather than flog yourself into continuing the binge because 'there's no hope,' CUT THE DRAMA!

Recognize what's happened, and even better, take time to look into yourself and the situation to possibly understand *why* it happened, and have mercy and gentleness for your being that is simply reverting to what it has known and what has worked in the past.

Just as we love our stories, we thrive on our drama. We tell ourselves the same pieces of information about ourselves over and over. It's no wonder we continue to fall off the wagon—we're the ones pushing ourselves off.

The drama dragon is insatiable. It has been fed continuously and voraciously by the media, by the opinions of our loved ones and others who are struggling with their own issues, and most importantly, by our own patterns.

If you stop feeding the dragon it will have to leave to find nourishment elsewhere. That's not your problem—your business is only you. Everyone has to deal with their own dragons. Others may try to unleash their own drama dragons on you, especially if you're not allowing them to feed their own through you, in the familiar patterns of the past. In fact, it's more common than not for their response to intensify.

That's not your business. Your business is only you—you and your dragon. You may have spent a long time together, but remember, dragons are not to be trusted. They only live to hide your treasure from you, by whatever means possible. Let them go.

Reflection

Position yourself comfortably in your quiet space. If writing appeals to you, have pen and paper ready, or better yet, a journal.

Close your eyes, and simply focus on your breath. Be aware of breathing in, breathing out, breathing in, breathing out, breathing in, breathing out.

The following questions or statements may be an aid to direct your inner work:

What is the strongest, deepest belief you have about yourself? Is it true? How do you know it's true?

Think of the beliefs you have about yourself, and for each one, think of the reasons why you know this belief to be true, or why it perhaps is not true.

For those that you think may not be true, reflect on how you would feel if you let go of that belief.

seventeen

We must embrace pain and burn it as fuel for our journey.

– Kenji Miyazawa

You start with a darkness to move through but sometimes the darkness moves through you.

– Dean Young

Pain is Our Teacher

It's a primal instinct to avoid pain. Our fight-or-flight response is innate and connected to our inherent need for survival. When faced with painful or frightening situations, whether they be physically or emotionally painful, our nervous systems react in preparation to take action if necessary: our heart beats quicker, our breathing becomes shallow and fast, our body tenses and contracts. All of these responses are warning signals and contradictory to the calm and equilibrium that nourishes our being.

Of course we want to avoid it and make it go away. Pain is inevitable and it is an integral aspect of the human condition, yet our society and the media stoke and fan the fire of the 'feel good' market, feeding our impulse to avoid pain at all costs.

It should be noted that there are those, however, who believe "Pain is inevitable, suffering is optional" and "Pain x Resistance = Suffering" (Shinzen Young). In this belief, our pain gets compounded by the amount of resistance we add to it. If we can allow its expression and observe it, we may be able to diffuse it or at the very least accept it equanimously without magnifying it.

Obviously, easier said than done in many cases.

But what are the possibilities?

Pain can be our teacher. Pain tells us when we are off track in some way—physically, emotionally, mentally or spiritually.

Pain has many faces, depending on what aspect of your being needs to be addressed.

Physical pain is often fairly obvious, and can be a result of overworking a muscle, moving or shifting in a way that jars your physical make-up, or it can be pain as a result of disease and illness.

Mental or spiritual pain can manifest in feelings of unease or discomfort, feeling 'off' or troubled about choices you're making or the way things are going.

Emotional pain has been a constant teacher in my life. It feels like I'm an expert in that area. Emotional pain manifests in so many ways. It's not surprising that in our society today, anxiety and depression are rampant and nearly everyone has trouble coping with the day-to-day of our existence.

And it's no wonder—we are encouraged and trained to repress and avoid any negative emotion, any psychological pain, any uncomfortable feelings: "Here, have a drink, it'll help you relax. Oh, have ten and you'll forget all about it!"

"Have a toke, it'll calm you down, make everything nice and fuzzy and okay."

"Take this antidepressant. It'll make you feel tranquil and even and FLAT, but 'fine,' and it'll be easier to get through each day."

"Take this upper, have an energy drink. It'll give you the boost you need and rev up your system to get through those next super-charged hours," when probably what your body really needs is rest.

It goes on and on.

We are constantly being conditioned to turn away, run away, escape at all costs (and the costs are huge) from our greatest Teacher.

In *Seeking the Heart of Wisdom*, Jack Kornfield speaks about the possibilities open to us when we choose to face our pain:

> When we allow ourselves to experience it fully and directly, we find that there opens all around this raw and hurting place a feeling of surprising spaciousness. When we don't add identification and reaction to it, the pain is just there, as it is, bearable... We have a hard time believing that we are actually able to face our own pain. We have convinced ourselves that it is something to fear and avoid at all costs. We have been conditioned to believe that, and so our society has been built around this fear... But there is no need to fear our pain... Facing it directly, we can come to freedom. (Kornfield 174 – 175)

Emotional pain does not go away if we choose to ignore it or suppress it. It becomes food for our dragons, those tenacious beings lurking below our consciousness, waiting to be triggered so they can roar out their existence and tear open our inner wounds.

Even before gaining the tools of body sensation awareness through Vipassana and having a regular two-hour-a-day meditation practice, I learned to spend time with my pain and allow its expression. If you let it speak, if you let it flow through you, you may find that it can be released. And yes, this can be daunting and scary at times, and maybe something you work through with a trained professional if your pain is overwhelmingly traumatic. This is your call; if the thought of facing this on your own is too intimidating, it may be in your best interest to seek help.

Those times when I was dealing with a lot of anger, or grief, or loss and sadness, I would find at least a half day—preferably a full day—when I could be alone in my home or in a secluded and safe place, and I would sit quietly, and open to my pain. I would invite it to speak to me, show me where it was coming from, reveal the different faces of its expression. And since journaling is my personal therapy, I would always have pen and paper in hand and I would write and write and write everything that was pouring out of me. And that's how it felt, like it was coming out of me—I was writing it out of me.

It would roar and I would scribble through my sobbing, and I would let it roar, and listen to what it was screaming, and have no judgement as to whether or not it made sense or was justified, just let it pour out and have its say. And sometimes I would be shaking with my anger, or collapsing in my sorrow, but it would pass.

It would pass.

And I was left exhausted, yet lighter, fuller, calmer, softer.

And I would destroy the evidence.

There's no need for others to see the harsh judgements that poured out of you, no need to inflict them with your raw and savage hurts. Your pain had its say, and hopefully that is enough for the time being. No doubt you will need to revisit it for processing—more than once—but generally that will not be as intense and painful as that initial release. But be prepared that the processing may continue for some time—days, weeks, years even—as you unwrap layers of yourself. It does get easier and gentler as you become less reactive and attached to it, and if you are committed to your personal growth, there is always more to learn.

Another way to start exploring and learning from your pain in a slower, hopefully more gentle process, is through meditation and any kind of mindful awareness techniques. Given that we spend so much time distracting ourselves with technology and all our screens, and all our sensual pleasures, and our incessant physical acquisitions ("Buy this!" "You must have this!" "How can you possibly live without this?!"), it is such a wonderful gift to start getting to know the you inside; to become aware of your present rather than being flooded by regrets of the past or overcome by worries of the future, to start hearing and trusting your own intuition and knowing what is right or what is wrong for YOU.

When I started this practice with that initial ten-day course in silence, many people responded with aversion: "Why would you choose to not talk for ten days? I'd *never* do that!"

And others responded with contemplative curiosity, intrigued by the challenge and the possibilities.

Of course it doesn't appeal to everyone. We are all at different places in our personal journeys and have our own methods and tools for navigating through life.

But there is such a gift in silence. It's incredibly difficult at first; most of us want to run out the door more than once during those ten days, even though we recognize that there's no real escape from ourselves. A silent retreat can be difficult at any time, even if it's your twentieth one, as it's not our norm. But to stop, and listen, and observe the process going on in our mind/body connection gives us insight into our choices and reactions and offers the possibility of creating positive change towards a calmer and more equilibrious state. We become empowered creators of our existence rather than chaotic casualties of our triggers.

Your pain can show you what you need to become aware of in order to grow. It's not an easy path. But then, most things that are worth having aren't. Otherwise we'd all be there.

We cannot avoid pain; it is a part of the human condition. We can, however, choose to allow our pain to direct us, inform us, and teach us.

And then, let it go.

It's another one of those pernicious dragons concealing our inner peace.

Let it have its say, and let it go.

Reflection

Position yourself comfortably in your quiet space. If writing appeals to you, have pen and paper ready, or better yet, a journal.

Close your eyes, and simply focus on your breath. Be aware of breathing in, breathing out, breathing in, breathing out, breathing in, breathing out.

The following questions or statements may be an aid to direct your inner work:

Think of a very painful situation. If you were able to let go of your pain around this, what would be left?

If you let go of your pain, what does that mean regarding those you feel are responsible for your pain?

How does that affect you moving forward, for yourself and for your relationship with them?

eighteen

We all have a story. The difference is: do you use the story to empower yourself? Or do you use your story to keep yourself a victim? The question itself empowers you to change your life.

– Sunny Dawn Johnston

You Are Not a Victim

When I decided to give up alcohol in order to preserve my family, my relationships and my overall health and sanity, I went through a period of feeling deprived. Naturally. No big surprise there.

Why could EVERYONE else enjoy a drink and have the option of loosening up in a social situation, but not me? Poor me—I could never enjoy a lovely glass of red wine with my meal, or a frosty cold beer on a hot summer day, or a frothy margarita on the beach, or bubbly champagne at a celebration, or yummy Bailey's in my coffee, or or or. . . The list goes on and on. And don't even think about going to an all-inclusive resort—absolute TORTURE!

Pot helped. At least I could adjust my attitude and get that relaxed high, and when I coupled that with a good non-alcoholic beer it was an okay alternative, and didn't cause me grief or get me into any trouble.

But my intoxicant of choice had been wine, and nothing can replace the savour and satisfaction of a good red wine; the non-alcoholic attempts are sorry and feeble imitations and not worth the disappointment. And I felt deprived.

It's taken me years to be okay with my choice.

And that's the key word—choice.

You are making a choice to live a better, richer, fuller life, a life that is empowering rather than defeating and debilitating. Rather than wallowing in your loss or deprivation or 'woe is me' attitude, think instead of the strength and positive perspective you are building. Applaud yourself daily, hourly, moment by moment, for your clarity and commitment to your life journey. And—in moderation—allow yourself those other sensory appetites that bring you pleasure and satisfaction, whether they be a sweet snack (repeat: in moderation), a hot bath, a special non-alcoholic beverage, a relaxing massage—satisfy your sensory craving in other ways.

You are not depriving yourself. You are rewarding your spirit that longs to be the best you, that knows there is a better and more fulfilling way to live.

Don't look for others to blame for your situation, nor expect others to 'fix' you. That is the epitome of the victim role. If you choose to foster that perspective, your hopes of bringing yourself to a happier state are pretty low.

If we refuse to accept responsibility for our state in life and instead lay guilt on others for not supplying or acquiescing to our needs and wants, we have little chance of achieving peace of mind or happiness.

There have been incidents in my life where I could have quite easily taken on the victim role, the two most obvious being the rape and then the financial and emotional theft by a con man during my twenties; in both cases, yes, I was a victim. But staying in that mindset does not lead to recovery or healing or moving forward, and I was able to work through those events with the help of professionals and friends and move on in my life.

It's interesting that feeling like a victim to my compulsive behaviours has been a much more difficult and complex and multi-layered hurdle that keeps recurring with different faces and in varying degrees. This just tells me that it is a very deep-seated thinking pattern that requires constant vigilance and consistent rewiring. . . and it is all up to me.

We are each our own creator, responsible for our attitudes, our relationships, our situations and our states of mind. No one 'owes' us anything, truly. We are the ones who need to start with whatever we have been given and work from there, whether it be in our job situation, our family interactions, our physical challenges, our compulsive behaviours. We each have our own obstacles and disadvantages and yes, some people seem to have fewer than others or more given to them than others. It's difficult to justify those imbalances at times. Perhaps there is truth to the idea of karma or past lives; that would make sense of the vast disparity present within our human conditions and circumstances. Since we cannot know the answer with any absolute certainty, why spend our precious lives being bitter and resentful about our particular situations? Why not take the hand we've been dealt and play it to our best advantage? And why look to others to do that for us?

There is no greater satisfaction than the empowerment of knowing you—within yourself and only yourself—are okay.

Life is full of chaos, hardships, devastation, cruelty, grief and injustice and it is also full of joy and beauty and friendship and connection and goals achieved, and love.

You may not be that one in a million person who will change the world, but you can be that one person who has learned to make the most within your circle, within that small piece of the world that each of us can influence and touch and wherein we can find and create meaning.

Most of us don't or can't 'have it all.' We all have our limitations and life circumstances which may determine our trajectory, and if we choose an attitude of seeing what we *can* have and do and achieve, as opposed to what we *can't* have or do or accomplish, our lives and our states of mind will be fuller and more rewarding. Don't look for others to give it to you or do it for you. There is no true sense of satisfaction or inner growth in manipulating someone to gratify your desires. It may feel that way momentarily, but that inner need for self-empowerment and well-being will never be met and that harmony within will forever be lacking.

We are here to connect and to support and help each other, but the true steps in personal growth are ours alone to take. And why give that power to someone else? Cherish your human heritage to grow and be and change, always changing, always being. And if you need to let go of something in order to take the next step, let it go with gratitude and move on, lighter, clearer, stronger.

There's no victim in this. There is only a victor, a survivor, a stronger you than the you that was.

Reflection

Position yourself comfortably in your quiet space. If writing appeals to you, have pen and paper ready, or better yet, a journal.

Close your eyes, and simply focus on your breath. Be aware of breathing in, breathing out, breathing in, breathing out, breathing in, breathing out.

The following questions or statements may be an aid to direct your inner work:

Write down all the reasons you can think of to feel sorry for yourself. Beside each one, write the sense of 'validation' you think you get from it:

Does it give you attention from others? Does it give you a release from responsibility? Does it give you a reason to blame others, or compare yourself to others?

Is this how you want to keep living?

How would you feel if you were able to let go of these thinking patterns?

nineteen

As our awareness of the world and who we are increases, we will grow to replace our needs with service, fear with love and scarcity with abundance.

— Joseph Rain,
The Unfinished Book About Who We Are

Retain / Replace / DEPRIVE

There are many different perspectives regarding how we manage our behaviours when we are trying to make change, and I don't believe any one of them is THE correct answer.

The correct answer is what works for you.

Twenty years after originally giving up alcohol cold turkey (and yes, there was a brief two-year relapse within that period when I *knew* I was strong enough/healed/over it and could *surely* drink socially—yeah, right. . .), I'm still enjoying non-alcoholic beer, often daily. It's my beverage of choice at a house party (I often BYOB it), when I'm out for dinner, and often at home as a pre-dinner drink or while cooking, much as I would have during my drinking days. I enjoy the taste, it's not a sugary beverage and it's generally low in calories. And best of all, it gives me the distinct pleasure of 'having a drink,' and yes, I still love that feeling. I just don't want the dire consequences and the reality distortion that alcohol brings.

And I still struggle with the feeling of deprivation. EVERYONE else can enjoy a drink or toke or party substance except me. Sound familiar? . . .yeah.

So I *don't* deprive myself. An alcoholic drink is NOT on the table (and if it is, it's not for me) but otherwise I get to have what I want. And this works—for me.

Most people in AA would strongly disagree. They feel the only recovery lies in completely changing your habits and your thinking. I agree that the thinking needs to change, but in my case I've found I've been able to retain a very pleasant treat without the debilitating repercussions.

It's the same philosophy I learned to help me get through bulimia in my early twenties. Diets and depriving myself of my favourite foods put me on this desperate roller coaster of being 'careful' and 'good' and avoiding 'bad' food and then BAM! Binging. And again, the self-deprecating remorse that followed, with vows to once again be 'good'—AAAH!

When I took a three-day intensive therapy workshop for eating disorders, much of the time was spent becoming aware of our inner pain or grief or loss—the reasons we may be over-eating—and the rest of the time was spent learning to have a new relationship with food. If you're dealing with loss in particular, taking away your favourite comfort foods *increases* your pain and emptiness. At least, that's how it is for me.

The first thing we were asked to do was to leave food on our plates at every meal. And that did not mean to pile on twice as much as we normally ate. We were to take our usual portions, and *always* leave something on our plate. This was really difficult for me at first, being

Retain / Replace / DEPRIVE

raised with European immigrants and the ironclad rule of finishing your plate, not wasting food and not having 'big eyes, little stomach.'

But this rule was crucial as part of the next and more difficult step: learning to listen to your body and recognize when it was full. Most of us overeat, especially in Western society where bigger is always better. The most obvious example is the horrendous 'Supersize' meals of McDonald's and other fast food organizations, but most of us eat far more than we need, and we eat for taste or boredom or comfort or distraction. And we most often eat past our 'full' barometer. The trick of leaving food on your plate is a visual clue to begin to notice when your body has had enough.

The other very important piece I learned in this workshop was to give myself my favourite foods; not to deprive myself of those foods that brought me comfort or pleasure, but to eat them until I was *full*, then stop. I could eat those same favourite foods later, once I was hungry again, but this perspective teaches some moderation without deprivation. You can satisfy your desires and cravings, and then STOP. . . until the next time.

There is no 'bad' food and no 'bad' behaviour if you learn to listen to your body.

I had to learn to apply this same perspective in other aspects of my life. Rather than view my desire for vegging in front of the TV as negative and needing to be cut out, I learned that I could still give myself permission to enjoy it without needing to be stoned or drunk to do so. Personally I still have an aversion to TV watching in the daytime, unless it's a snowed-in day or there's a special game or marathon on, but I love my evenings of dinner and munchies while enjoying a few hours of my favourite programs—guilt-free.

So, contrary to some beliefs that it is necessary to remove those behaviours that are associated with the substance abuse, over the years I chose to change my perspective towards them, and retain the benefits they provided, learning moderation (YES!) along the way.

Granted, I also developed new habits and comforting behaviours: yoga became my exercise of choice to bring me into my body and give this miraculous organism the gratification and benefits it needs to function and flourish. My dog blessed me with the fulfillment of long walks alone yet not alone, and the well-being they provide, and I am forever grateful to her. A hot bath and a good book at the end of the day are as good as an episode of Survivor and bag of Cheetos—some days you want one combo, and some days you want the other.

A wonderful wise woman in my Monday morning meditation group blessed me with a pivotal and critical key within this process. One morning I shared that I was having difficulty in getting rid of behaviours that were detrimental and no longer serving me. She said that these behaviours *had* served me, to bring me to this point in my life, and had benefited me in some way to be able to achieve that purpose. Rather than despise them or try to cut them out of my life, I should embrace them, be grateful to them for bringing me this far and then let them go gently, with love and grace, as I continued forward to new changes and new behaviours.

If we continue hating ourselves, or parts of ourselves, we cannot heal. It is in letting go in grace and harmony and gratitude that we acknowledge and embrace all our truths, in order to move forward to our new truths.

Let those dragons go gently, with gratitude for their service, and wish them well.

Reflection

Position yourself comfortably in your quiet space. If writing appeals to you, have pen and paper ready, or better yet, a journal.

Close your eyes, and simply focus on your breath. Be aware of breathing in, breathing out, breathing in, breathing out, breathing in, breathing out.

The following questions or statements may be an aid to direct your inner work:

What do you feel you are missing out on? In what areas are you deprived? What comes up within when you feel deprived?

Are these things you're missing important to your survival? How are they crucial to your well-being or your ability to function day-to-day and in relationships?

What things or activities bring you comfort? Are you able to keep them in moderation in your life, or is it more beneficial to find new comforts?

twenty

Fall seven times, stand up eight.

— Japanese proverb

Relapse

Step 1 – DO NOT BEAT YOURSELF UP!

Step 2 – Accept that you are human with the best of intentions and NOT infallible.

Step 3 – Accept your choice and your present state. It is your present Truth.

Step 4 – Accept, too, that this may not be your only relapse in your journey to change.

Step 5 – DO NOT BEAT YOURSELF UP!

It's not easy. In fact, this change you've chosen is one of the most difficult and courageous endeavours. When we are poked by those deep-seated triggers, we're not always able to resist, ignore or work our way through them and past them.

My deepest and most ingrained trigger is the cottage. Ah, the cottage—the Place of Permission, the ultimate chill haven, la-la land. Nowhere to go, nowhere I have to be, nothing really that I have to do. I'd tuck in there with all my favorite indulgences—foods, drinks, books, games, movies and—in the past—my favourite substance(s).

It's *really* hard for me to be straight at the cottage. It's been the relapse trigger more often than anything else. In fact, I am writing this at the cottage in the midst of a relapse after more than fourteen weeks of clear and confident abstaining, thinking this was it—this was my 'forever' quitting time. Sigh.

What happened? The first cottage stay of the season. That's it, that's all. No major trauma, no major anxiety—other than the thought of intense deprivation without my familiar means of escape. Although, I had noticed a deep indefinable sadness the previous few weeks and I could not get to the source of it, nor could I shake it off. And I didn't like it. As much as I say I welcome pain and discomfort as opportunities to grow, hell no. I don't like it. Equanimity? Easier said than felt.

Maybe that sadness was leading me deeper into myself, into the reasons why. Maybe if I'd stayed with it, in it, accepted it, held it, it may have led me to the next plateau.

And maybe that sadness was a sense of loss, loss of that familiar companion, that comforting cure. It was more intense the closer I got to cottage time.

And there *is* a loss, no question. When you have relied on something to get you through the tough times, the hurt, the sadness, the anger, the boredom, the stress, but also the good times, to help celebrate the highs, the achievements, the holidays, the milestones, the cottage times—when you have depended on this your whole adult life, it's a loss. There is a void, and there is change. It's not comfortable.

We are conditioned to make our discomfort go away by the quickest means possible. Going straight is choosing the opposite: it's choosing the discomfort, facing it head on, looking your shit in the face.

Anyway, that was it—the cottage pushed me over the edge.

Relapse

Truly, it's a bit baffling. I seem to be able to handle many other difficult and stressful situations, but put me at the cottage with no 'party' and I'm angry, resentful, depressed and deprived and really feeling sorry for myself.

And the 'pity party' is not the party I want.

So, the next step—Step 6—is to begin to know mercy and kindness and gentleness—for yourself.

None of us are 'perfect' in anything. In the words of the wonderful Elizabeth Gilbert, renowned author of Eat, Pray, Love:

> So, for anyone out there who is 'failing' at being the perfect caregiver, the perfect mother, the perfect wife, the perfect friend, [the perfect recovering addict]…please drop the knife you are holding at your own throat. It was never your job to be the perfect ANYTHING. Your only job is to find mercy—starting with you. Again and again and again. (Gilbert)

Again and again and again. Mercy—for myself. Because I am not a bad person.

I do, however, choose the easier road at times. When I get stretched far in my new skin, and when the change has me feeling taut to the point of splitting, I don't like it and I want to step back into my familiar shape. I'm not giving up or saying it's over. Just curling up with my old friend for a bit, taking a breather, and then I'll start again.

But here's the problem: each time you pull back from that rending, splitting, dissevering, really uncomfortable stretch, you snap back into your old self. You need to take a deep breath and just GO THERE. Stay there. Stay with it. STRETCH. And it will become more comfortable, more known, more familiar.

You have to grow into that new shape, that new skin, and it's *not* comfortable. It's *not* known. It's *not* familiar. Not at first. But the more you walk in it, the better it will feel.

Reflection

Position yourself comfortably in your quiet space. If writing appeals to you, have pen and paper ready, or better yet, a journal.

Close your eyes, and simply focus on your breath. Be aware of breathing in, breathing out, breathing in, breathing out, breathing in, breathing out.

The following questions or statements may be an aid to direct your inner work:

Reflect on the steps of your relapse. What was the trigger? How were you feeling just prior to this, or in thinking about the situation before you headed into it? Did you subconsciously give yourself permission to cave if triggered?

How did you treat yourself post-relapse? Was your 'morning after' the same as multitudes of previous times of remorse and self-abuse or were you able to be gentler and more forgiving of yourself?

Can you forgive yourself now? Can you offer yourself empathy and compassion, knowing how difficult this is and how hard you are trying?

What steps can you put in place to set yourself up for a different outcome in the future?

What healthy rewards or enjoyment can you give yourself for making new and different choices?

Sacred Path Card #25
Pow – Wow

If the Talking Drums have signaled a Pow-Wow, you are being put on notice to gather together with others of like mind and exchange ideas. The quickening of some aspect of your life will be aided if you use a support system and see what type of support you can call upon from others.

The Pow-Wow card is marking a time of calling in your markers. You may need assistance or just a friend to be a sounding board. Your focus will become clearer, and you may receive the boost you need just from an encouraging word or two.

The quickening is inside of you and speaks of the time just preceding birth. Whatever you are giving birth to at this time can be assisted by gathering your friends around you for the needed support. (Sams 200 – 201)

twenty-one

Courage doesn't always roar. Sometimes courage is the quiet voice at the end of the day saying, 'I will try again tomorrow.'

— Mary Anne Radmacher

Start Again

In the Vipassana practice as taught by S.N. Goenka, he often repeats this gentle encouragement:

"Start again."

He uses this as a reminder when our undisciplined 'monkey mind' keeps pulling us away from our focus and into the crazy chaos of endless chatter within. If you have ever taken up any mindfulness practice, then you are well aware of the incessant insanity within our minds, the stories we delve into and repeat and reaffirm, the conversations we create about what we should have said last time or what we're going to say next time, the regret from past decisions that we replay and rehash, the anxiety and scenarios of our 'what if' imaginings—the list is endless. The mind never stops.

I like to compare my mind's undisciplined behaviour to that of a puppy, needing gentle, consistent and loving reminders so that it has the potential to grow into a loyal and beneficial companion. We teach our exuberant puppy to "Sit. . . stay!" just as we teach our mind, over and over again, to sit with and stay with the thoughts that will lead to healing and moving forward. And rather than berating our puppy mind, we bring it back each time with love and compassion for our efforts. How can you beat up a puppy?

An essential aspect of Vipassana or insight meditation is to become aware of this penchant of the mind, to observe the impermanence of our thoughts without reacting and to bring our awareness to the reality of the present moment—again and again and again.

Start again, every few minutes, every few seconds, if that's the case, with no inner recriminations, no feeling badly at your ineptitude. Goenka says, "Smilingly, bring yourself back, and start again."

Even saying the word 'smilingly' brings a smile to your face, and when we smile, we inadvertently soften—it's a tangible shift.

And so can you, on your path to recovery and changing your behaviour patterns, smilingly, start again, and again, and again.

When I was younger, starting again meant drastically changing my course of action: quitting a job, ending a relationship, moving across the country. Shortly after the rape violation I did just that. The need to 'start again' was overwhelming, and it needed to be big, and tangible, and I needed to find some sense of safety which wasn't happening in the city where the violation occurred. So I quit my job, packed up my 1973 blue Capri and started driving west with a tent and sleeping bag for my accommodations. It took a month to drive over 4,000 kilometres as I took my time, visiting a couple friends along the way but mostly guarding my solitude as I sought some reprieve from the fear that saturated my being.

But of course, I brought all of it with me. It takes time for us to learn that running away from our issues doesn't work; the cloud just follows us to the next location. It would be many years before I could soften to that place of fear within me and accept it and allow it to pass through when it showed its face and to know that it would not last if I allowed it to pass. Starting again for me now is an inner shift and an exercise to examine my thought patterns and perspectives in order to create change.

Soften within, embrace your struggling, bumbling, erring humanity, and start again. Every new start is one step further ahead. There is no shame in needing to start again; there is new hope and new resolve and new energy and new strength.

Every moment is new. In every moment we are being renewed; our present cells are dying, and new cells are being created.

Our old thoughts, too, can 'die,' and new thoughts can replace them.

Each time you start again, you're starting from a different place. 'Start again' does not mean you are returning to the 'start' position; we are not runners in a race or an obstacle course having to go back to the beginning when we falter.

You've made changes, even if they are too small for you to recognize at the time; you've altered something within your pattern, because for a period of time, you were reacting differently. Your mind/body will remember that, and you will start again from that new place.

Our bodies do this re-creation intrinsically, not needing any conscious input on our part, whereas our minds, left to their own devices, will inherently struggle *against* our efforts to 'start again.' They do not want to change. They prefer the familiarity of previous patterns, and the ease and comfort of falling into those well-rooted ruts.

This is why our triggers can so easily and instantly trip us up. I don't know how many times I've mindlessly reached for the joint innocently offered during a social engagement after days or weeks of abstinence. It's like all my resolve and efforts never existed and certainly don't matter at the time; it's a reflex that feels completely right and acceptable at that moment.

Therein lies our 'work.' We are filling those reflexive ruts with new and fresh soil, sometimes doing so even while carrying the heavy rocks and boulders of the old beliefs we fear letting go though they bend our backs with the heaviness of their deception. And I say deception because they are not true within themselves. We have beliefs about ourselves and who we are because that is what we've been telling ourselves, what our *past* actions have reinforced within us.

Toss off those unnecessary burdens of your past. They are not serving you, only trapping you and binding you to the same patterns of thinking that have kept you stagnant in your self-concept.

Everything changes, and SO DO YOU.

Innately we are aware of this, hence the urge for new starts, New Year's resolutions, 'new moon, new me' impulses. This is the Truth of our existence—we are *all* starting again at every moment, and every time we step back into those familiar ruts is another opportunity to start again. Hopefully each time there is more dumping of the old beliefs and less of a rut to dip into, but regardless, start again, my friend. Smilingly, softly, gently, start again, from this new place.

Start again with compassion for your struggles, with empathy for our shared experiences, with gratitude for each new step you are taking, and with equanimity for each new awareness, no matter if it's pleasant or painful. The conscious path of change and growth is a difficult and challenging road. Smilingly, start again, and celebrate every step.

Reflection

Smilingly, Start Again.
You can do this.

twenty-two

You are the bows from which your children as living arrows are sent forth.

— Khalil Gibran, *The Prophet*

Being a Role Model

Nothing in my life has been more fulfilling, rewarding, heart-breaking, educating, agonizing and absolutely purely joyful than being a parent. To embark on that journey is by far the best choice I made. To know another soul from the moment of inception, and to have the honour of being a crucial instrument in their development...it's a humbling and intensely gratifying venture and adventure.

When I first became a mom I was still drinking; not during pregnancy or breastfeeding, but pretty much from the moment my body was once again my own, the party was back on. Of course, with my new and very serious responsibilities, I tried to be more moderate, but anyone who has battled with alcohol knows how cunning, insidious and immoral it can be. It cares not whether you might be compromising your loved ones' safety, but just keeps pushing that more-is-better button.

I remember that it was April 1999, Easter weekend, when I decided enough was enough. Up until that time, Easter was always a slippery slope for me. Growing up with Polish immigrants as parents and grandparents gave me a lovely, robust and hearty culture that I embrace to this day. But, part of their 'robust and hearty' attributes often include a propensity toward heavy drinking in any and all social situations, and given that our Easter Sunday celebration started with a Catholic 6:00 am sunrise service, the celebrations and socializing began immediately after. By 8:30 am, we were all around the breakfast table with 'waker-uppers' of vodka and orange juice or the more traditional rye shots to toast the day. And it only continued from there, with the pinochle cards coming out after breakfast, and another bottle of Five Star whiskey on the table (as kids we would collect the shiny gold stars as tokens). It would be a twelve-hour marathon before the day was done.

Now, not everyone would get shit-faced. They had amazing tolerance for alcohol and it was rare that I would see my parents or my aunts and uncles really drunk. But as I grew older and attained drinking age, this was a great opportunity for a no-holds-barred all-out drink fest. Easter Monday was always a really, really rough day . . .

The day I chose to stop drinking was Easter Monday. The night before I'd stayed up drinking after putting the kids to bed. At that time I was also still smoking cigarettes. I passed out on the couch and became conscious a few hours later with a large burn in the coffee table from a lit cigarette that had fallen out of the ashtray.

That was enough.

That was enough to smack me across the head and realize I could not let this go further, to the point where I could do serious harm to my children through my drunken negligence.

I didn't care enough about myself to stop, but I did love them beyond measure and was at least wise enough to know I didn't need to go any further to rock bottom and have to deal with irresponsible and irreversible tragedy.

Being a Role Model

I came back to this same place with my pot-smoking. Granted, marijuana is a far less harmful drug. It doesn't make you completely reckless, or violent, or stupid, or heedless, or volatile. I never felt I was putting my children or myself in danger when I was smoking. What was happening, however, was an increasing lethargy and muddled sense of what I should and could be doing.

On one hand, marijuana helped me cope in a difficult marriage that I wasn't ready to leave, for the sake of my children. It helped me to live with the anger and resentment and sadness in order to keep going enough to maintain the status quo and still enjoy some good family years.

And it was interesting that when I first stopped smoking weed and was completely straight for about eighteen months, once the 'smoke' cleared, I realized I could not remain in the marriage for the sake of my own dying spirit. My children were older; one was leaving for university and both could make the decision of where they chose to live without being forced to share their time between two households.

I realized that I wasn't role-modelling the kind of behaviour I wanted to for their potential growth. I wasn't role-modelling a healthy relationship.

To be fair, role modelling was something I lacked growing up. My parents were fine people who did the best they could, but unfortunately theirs was a relationship of endurance rather than mutual affection and respect, not uncommon in the 1950s and 1960s. You married and you stayed married and you 'made it work,' even if it turned you into a bitter, resentful person who grew to hate your partner. You carried on 'appearances.'

I watched this growing up and vowed I would never follow that example. And when I saw myself becoming an angry, bitter, resentful person—once the 'smoke' cleared and I wasn't numbing my pain and unhappiness—I knew this was not the example I wanted to show my daughters. Why would I force myself to stay in a situation that I would never wish for another? And I am grateful to my mother who supported me through my separation, having regretted her own decision to 'stick it out.'

As a child there were really no female role models I wanted to emulate. Being raised with three older brothers—wonderful people, but not females—I muddled my way through, bouncing off walls through my young adult years, somehow finding my way through with helpful literature, counselling and good friends.

It has always been a goal to be the best possible role model for my daughters, my stepdaughters and step-grandkids, my students, and all the young people whose lives I've touched over the years.

In order to be a role model, one must first walk the steps and climb to those aspirations oneself. How can you show the way if you have not yet walked the way?

If I could not first find enough *self*-love to treat myself more kindly and reach that 'potential' I could always feel within, at least my love for my children—that strongest, deepest, most all-encompassing, never-ending love we feel for our children—at least *that* love motivated me. I am forever grateful to my daughters for so many reasons, and that is one of them. Because of them, I have pushed through many of my own insecurities, issues, struggles, and negative behaviour patterns in order to help them; in order for them to also see what is possible, what one can work through, what strength lies within, what support is there for you.

I have to do it myself if I want to show it to them and be there for them in that capacity. Anything else will not ring true.

And as time has carried on, Life in its infinite wisdom and circle of learning has turned my daughters into my role models. My older daughter exemplifies love and caring for all, never leaving anyone behind, and is achieving her own dreams with a consistent, steady perseverance and resilience that humbles me. The wisdom and authenticity of my younger daughter has at times stopped me in my tracks and struck gold in my own quest for truth.

Find your strength within, find whatever motivates you to be your best self. If you cannot yet find that love within yourself, find that love for something or someone else that will carry you through your struggles and changes and steps necessary to get to that better place, that happier self.

We are always our Truth, and still we always have more truth, other truths to reach for, to grow into, to become, to light the way for ourselves and for others.

As the insightful Elizabeth Gilbert says, "Be who you needed when you were younger" (Gilbert).

Reflection

Position yourself comfortably in your quiet space. If writing appeals to you, have pen and paper ready, or better yet, a journal.

Close your eyes, and simply focus on your breath. Be aware of breathing in, breathing out, breathing in, breathing out, breathing in, breathing out.

The following questions or statements may be an aid to direct your inner work:

At this point in your life, what impression are you leaving for others? How would you be remembered?

Think of someone who has been a role model for you. What is it about them that you would like to emulate?

How would you like to be remembered?

twenty-three

On one side of accountability is courage, on the other is freedom.

– Jean Hamilton-Fford, *Play.Create.Succeed*

It is not only what we do, but also what we do not do, for which we are accountable.

– Jean-Baptiste Poquelin (Moliére)

Accountability

You are walking the hero's journey. In the archetype of the hero, much of the journey is spent in solitude and inner struggles and self-talk to persevere no matter the pain and difficulty. But the hero also has friends and guides along the way, because we are together in our journeys on this planet as much as we walk alone.

There is immeasurable relief and support to be gained from being able to share our struggle with others. As my brother says, "Shared pain is half pain. Shared joy is double joy."

Accountability is an integral piece of the path to change or recovery. It is so very easy to lose our momentum and fall back to familiar and easy behaviours. Putting a plan in place beforehand and having others to reach out to can help navigate those unexpected triggers that can easily trip us up.

One of the best support systems for staying with your path and staying accountable is having a friend as a sponsor. This has always been practiced in Alcoholics Anonymous, as they are well aware of how easy it is to take that first drink, and how important it is to have someone to reach out to, who understands and has been there. Someone whom you can contact at any time of day, because we never know when that spring will snap. And those snaps are relentlessly powerful and often out of the blue, especially in the beginning.

Is there a person you trust, someone who truly wishes for your well-being and understands your struggle enough to be as non-judgemental as possible? Are you able to open up to them and ask for their help?

Another powerful aid can be found in community support groups. These are especially helpful if you are unable to open up to someone close to you. There is often enough anonymity for members to feel safe in revealing their struggles, and there is something liberating and comforting in finding others who are going through similar difficulties and share stories that are as awful or even worse than yours. It helps us to realize we are not alone in our secretive self-destruction. This shared pain can lessen the heaviness in your heart and darkness in your self-concept.

Alcoholics Anonymous is one of the community support groups that offers incredible and consistent aid for so many. I remember the first couple of meetings I attended during that second trip down alcoholism lane when I'd been sure I could 'handle' it 'this time.' I walked into a couple church basements and could barely restrain myself from bolting out the door before the end of the meeting. This was NOT my tribe! No way!

At least, not at first. I did a little more research and found a local AA women's group and from the first meeting I attended, I felt a strong

Accountability

connection and mutual acceptance. This became my group for a long period, and I am so very grateful to these amazing women. They showed me that no matter our previous choices, we could accept ourselves and love ourselves, and live with grace and dignity and self-worth. I was proud and honoured to be a part of their tribe. Each weekly meeting brought more letting go of detrimental beliefs and new insights and further steps along the path, and it was so very helpful to have these lovely friends to contact when needed, any time of day or night (triggers don't have socially acceptable time frames or boundaries). Finding your tribe, your sangha, your community, and being able to share your struggles and stories is empowering and integral to maintaining your path.

Another step towards being accountable is to share your decision with others, especially those with whom you've partied in the past.

Very scary step. And yet, it often needs to happen sooner rather than later. Quite often these are your oldest and best friends, and it's pretty difficult to avoid them forever or pretend that everything's status quo.

Be prepared to be "Mexican-crabbed."

I will never forget a story I first heard in the teachings of the meditation group of my late teens. It's called the "Mexican crab" story, and I've often found variations of it since. Here is one version:

> On one sunny afternoon a man was walking along the beach and saw another man fishing in the surf with a bait bucket beside him. As he drew closer, he saw that the bait bucket had no lid and had live crabs inside. "Why don't you cover your bait bucket so the crabs won't escape?" he asked. "You don't understand," the man replied, "If there is one crab in the bucket it would surely crawl out very quickly. However, when there are many crabs in the bucket, if one tries to crawl up the side, the others will grab hold of it and pull it back down so that it will share the same fate as the rest of them." (Kuja)

If your partying friends are fine with their own lifestyle and behaviours (and more so, if they're NOT, yet are too afraid to attempt change) they may be quite vocal and persuasive in their arguments about why you're 'okay' and not needing to change.

Telling others is a very courageous and intimidating step, as then you will want to save face and maintain your goal. And should you falter, others will know. Yup, it's one of the ultimate accountabilities.

But for some of us, it is still too scary to allow someone else to see our struggle, to open up and reveal our shame and guilt. We know we need to change, but are not yet able to share this secret pain. How then can we be accountable?

Baby steps. And baby steps are still steps.

Try journaling. It will help you to be accountable to yourself. It's one thing to become aware of your thoughts, and it's another step entirely to physically manifest them on paper. There is something very accountable in being open and honest and *seeing* your thoughts on paper right in front of you. Not only does this help you to face yourself and look your shit in the face, it also creates a record of your progress and your journey and your celebratory moments. So if you're feeling too raw or too vulnerable to open up to anyone else, at least you're taking the first step in being real with yourself.

Set small goals for yourself. How many days would you like to try first? Maybe just a week, or maybe just getting through that first weekend without indulging in that familiar pattern. One step at a time.

Give yourself a reward for every time you make it to one of your goals. There *must* be celebrations because, trust me, there will be *many* difficult moments. You need to balance those with pleasure, give yourself a reason to walk through that difficult time to reach the light on the other side. And if previously your go-to self-talk has been mainly negative and abusive, there is a real need to start rewiring and celebrating yourself, nurturing yourself, loving yourself. You are so worth it.

Reach out and grab a hand, reach in and pull yourself up, reach further and keep walking.

Reflection

Position yourself comfortably in your quiet space. If writing appeals to you, have pen and paper ready, or better yet, a journal.

Close your eyes, and simply focus on your breath. Be aware of breathing in, breathing out, breathing in, breathing out, breathing in, breathing out.

The following questions or statements may be an aid to direct your inner work:

What would it feel like to share your story with someone?

Write down what you would say if you were to confide in someone in order to help stay accountable.

What would you say to yourself to celebrate reaching a goal? How would you reward yourself?

twenty-four

Friendship . . . is born at that moment when one man says to another, 'What! You too? I thought no one but myself. . .'

— C.S. Lewis, *The Four Loves*

In everyone's life, at some time, our inner fire goes out. It is then burst into flame by an encounter with another human being. We should all be thankful for those people who rekindle the inner spirit.

— Albert Schweitzer

Find Your Sangha

Sangha is a Sanskrit word meaning association, community, assembly, or company, and in Buddhism refers to a monastic community of monks or nuns.

I most often hear this word in reference to a spiritual or supportive community. Your sangha are the like-minded people who support you on your spiritual path or personal growth journey. For most of us, it's difficult to maintain this path without them. While it is true that you and you alone are responsible for taking each step in your journey, it is crucial to walk with others. Making change in our lives is one of the most difficult undertakings and so difficult to maintain. Getting started is often one of the easier steps; we all have experienced those 'new day, new me' moments, usually born from a regretful recent behaviour pattern or occurrence, and that initial resolve is nothing short of euphoric. Of course you're going to change! Why wouldn't you? You'd be stupid to continue down this same path when you're groveling in the mire of a transgression. The need for change is crystal clear and so very obvious at these points. You set a plan of action and you have a skip in your step and a newfound outlook on life. . . which lasts what—a month? A week? A day?

Change is difficult.

We need support along the way. We need to be able to share our experience—our fears and our despair and our shame and our regrets—and know that we're still okay and not the worst person in the world, that others have had similar experiences and can empathize with us. And we need to celebrate our victories, no matter how miniscule, and be validated by someone who completely understands the struggle and commitment needed for each tiny step. We learn the importance of being supported and in supporting others; together we help each other stay the course and get past the triggers and avoid the ruts.

The unfortunate truth within this is that sometimes it means seeing less of friends or relationships that have fostered your previous behaviours, at least in the beginning stages when you're feeling fragile in your resolve. Not only that, you may have to explain and defend your new understandings and recent intention to these friends, often suffering well-meaning interpretations of how you *should* handle this (which can include maintaining the shared behaviour and defending its 'merits' or minimizing its dangers), or enduring ridicule for hoping your situation can change. And yes, these are your loved ones speaking. Understand that they are dealing with their own fears and

Find Your Sangha

limitations—and the threat of losing you—but also not wanting to admit their own sense of futility or despair.

And it's not only those around us who may try to keep us from changing and growing. We all fear change, and our egos are constantly battling to maintain the status quo and keep us in our place.

This is when you need to branch out and find your like-minded people, your new tribe, your sangha. It doesn't mean you have to necessarily join a group or go to AA religiously, nor does it mean you have to cut off relations with all your present friends. It means you do have to make a consistent effort and be open to finding those who will support you and walk alongside you on your new path. Sometimes these individuals are found in a community support group, or at an AA meeting, or within a meditation practice. The more you reach out to try other options, the more possibility you have of finding your sangha.

When I have the opportunity to be with like-minded people, I notice that there is an openness and lightness and freer flow of energy within my whole being. It's like my entire body relaxes and sighs happily and OPENS. And on those occasions when I have a one-on-one with certain friends, the energy flow is visceral. It's like we open into each other, recharging our spirits, resonating within with each chord of our conversation. I leave the interaction feeling stronger, fuller, bigger somehow. It's palpable, and I no longer question it, but simply relish within it and am grateful.

As said previously, part of my struggle to maintain sobriety and abstinence from substance stems from the fear of not being 'cool.' Now I realize that the 'coolness' is a façade to cover the need for the crutch. And I say this with no judgement: it is a crazy chaotic and often very cruel world we are all trying to navigate through, and we all have our crutches, our coping behaviours and survival tactics that have successfully (or not) carried us this far.

Today, some of those individuals who are the 'coolest' and now my role models are those who manage to live their lives contributing to their communities without the use of detrimental substances or behaviours to keep going forward. And it's super cool if you were one of those with a crutch like an addiction or a compulsive substance abuse and you have managed to let it go and thrive without it. You are my superhero!

If you are struggling with substance abuse or a compulsive behaviour pattern, I strongly suggest looking for those who were once in your shoes. Chances are you will find your sangha, or at least one or two like-minded individuals with whom you resonate and can grow and walk alongside to support each other.

When I was working my way through my second bout with alcohol, through the AA women's group I joined a smaller and more intimate Twelve Step group. One of our members invited us into her home each week, and the eight of us would come together to work through the Twelve Step program (based on the AA edition, *Twelve Steps and Twelve Traditions*, Anonymous) and share our stories and our pain and our victories and our struggles and our accomplishments. I cherish those women and am so grateful to have had the opportunity to spend that time with them.

As time went on in my personal journey, I felt the need to connect with women to share more than our alcohol or addiction-related experiences. At that time I had reconnected with a former student with whom I'd been quite close during her years in high school, and it was such a pleasant surprise to know that connection was still there, but on a different and more equal level as I was no longer her teacher. And it amazed me that, though I was twice her age, there was never a feeling of separation because of this—an example of how age is just a number and our inner spirit is ageless. There was a lovely exchange of experience and knowledge from our different perspectives.

We seem to have turned away from the value in intergenerational support and interaction in our present society. Our elders are often shut away from us in old age homes where they have little possibility of interaction with other age groups. And as a high school teacher, I never underestimated the insight and new perspectives I gained in discussions with my students. There is such value in the exchange across generations; we can learn so much from each other as our race continues to evolve.

It was this framework of thought that sparked my former student and me to create the 'Women's Group.' We began to invite those we thought could benefit or contribute to a monthly evening of sharing our stories. Our ages ranged from nineteen to eighty-five, and the group was very fluid; sometimes there would be four of us together, sometimes twelve or fourteen. Occasionally there would be an initial topic of conversation—anxiety in group settings, climate change, an upcoming election, whatever sparked our interest—but most often each evening would become whatever it needed to be at that particular time, and the conversation would evolve on its own. It was quite magical, and so inspiring, and empowering, and rejuvenating for our spirits.

If you can't find your sangha, you can create it. It can be whatever you want it to be. It is so important to connect with like-minded people in order to continue your own journey. Yes, we need to take our own steps, but it is easier and less scary when you know you're not alone in your thinking.

They say we are most like the five people with whom we spend the most time. Who are you spending the majority of your time with? Are these people you respect, truly appreciate and would like to emulate? Or do they 'accept' all your shortcomings to help you stay mired in your cesspool of compulsive and detrimental craving?

It's not easy making these changes. It takes real courage to face your shadow side. We all have our areas where growth and change can result in a happier life, and it is only when we are ready to admit there is a need for change that it can begin. Not only do you have to have your eyes and mind and heart open to look your shit in the face, you then have to be ready to start digging, and to wake and face those sleeping dragons that have been covertly hiding the treasures of yourself that wait beneath.

Your sangha awaits. Go, find them, talk with them, walk with them.

Reflection

Position yourself comfortably in your quiet space. If writing appeals to you, have pen and paper ready, or better yet, a journal.

Close your eyes, and simply focus on your breath. Be aware of breathing in, breathing out, breathing in, breathing out, breathing in, breathing out.

The following questions or statements may be an aid to direct your inner work:

Which of your friends or family members may be most unsupportive if you make changes in your lifestyle? What might their reactions be?

For each possible reaction, can you think of a response now, to help you in future encounters?

How would it feel if you needed to make changes in the time and activities spent with your present social group?

What are the character traits and supportive behaviours that you think would be helpful in a sangha to help your chosen personal growth?

Where might you find like-minded people, your tribe?

twenty-five

Our authentic power is found in our truth. This is the place that shows us how to give what is so very good about ourselves.

— Jeanne McElvaney, *Old Maggie's Spirit Whispers*

Be Your Own Mrs. Dubose

You may already be smiling and nodding upon reading the title above, and if so, I smile with you.

If not, perhaps this will jog a memory—*To Kill A Mockingbird*. Right there at the top of my all-time favourite books, *To Kill A Mockingbird* by Harper Lee has a secondary character who has always maintained a place in my 'Role Models I Aspire To' Top Ten. Okay, maybe not the Top Ten, because, let's face it, Mrs. Henry Lafayette Dubose is a mean, cantankerous old bitch who takes bitter satisfaction in tormenting children with her racist lies and abuse. But she's been a role model for me because she chooses to overcome her morphine addiction as one of the last things she does before she dies.

Unfortunately, another thing she does before her death is antagonize the two Finch children, Jem and Scout, because their father, Atticus Finch, is defending a black man who is accused of raping a white woman. Her demeaning racial slurs are too much for twelve-year-old Jem and in a fit of rage he destroys the camellia bushes she loves.

As punishment, his father insists Jem read to Mrs. Dubose every afternoon after school, to help take her mind off her morphine withdrawal, and more so to learn a valuable lesson:

> I wanted you to see something about her—I wanted you to see what real courage is, instead of getting the idea that courage is a man with a gun in his hand. It's when you know you're licked before you begin but you begin anyway and you see it through no matter what. You rarely win, but sometimes you do. Mrs. Dubose won, all ninety-eight pounds of her. According to her views, she died beholden to nothing and nobody. She was the bravest person I ever knew. (Lee ch.11)

We can all be a Mrs. Dubose. And yup, it takes gut-wrenching courage.

If you have struggled with any kind of substance abuse or other compulsive behaviours, it is usually pretty clear who or what controls your power.

And this is not only true in alcohol consumption. Any kind of binging and compulsive excess—overeating, gambling, compulsive spending—can indicate that we are 'beholden' to something other than our best and truest selves.

Our paths may all be slightly different, our numbing comforts varied, and our timelines inconsistent, yet it all comes down to giving our personal pain all the power—it calls the shots and decides whether you'll drink that shot, and the next one, and the next one...

It is not an easy choice, but remember that your depth of suffering may be determined by how much power you feed it. If you are able to face those moments when your pain or your grief can sucker punch you into doubling over, and you let them pass through you, you can release them, bit by bit. As Elizabeth Gilbert says, "The posture that you take is you hit your knees in absolute humility and you let it rock you until it is done with you. And it will be done with you, eventually. And when it is done, it will leave" (Popova).

Until the next time. And there will be a next time, because being alive means that we're always facing discomfort and pain as much as we are enjoying pleasure and contentment. The more you practise allowing pain's expression, and letting it go through you, the more you can trust that you will be okay on the other side.

Mrs. Dubose chose a fast and furious cold turkey approach as her death was imminent; she didn't have time to flounder or have relapses or change her mind. My journey has been nearly five decades of ups and downs and short-lived sobriety and falling off the wagon and modifications and 'new day, new me' moments—over and over and over again. There have been baby steps and giant steps and backward steps and sideways steps and face plants and plateaus.

It doesn't matter. Every step counts. Every effort matters. If you want to make the change, you will, in your time and at your pace.

If you are familiar with *To Kill A Mockingbird* and the ordeal of Mrs. Dubose, you'll remember that she went through a frightening, painful and debilitating physical withdrawal. For many of us, the withdrawal is not just physical, but emotional and mental, and long term, as we work through and process all the layers we've gathered to defend ourselves from our triggers and pain.

Had she lived, I have no doubt that Mrs. Dubose would have had to work through withdrawal of a psychological nature, but she was successful in her goal of overcoming the physical dependency on the drug.

What is your goal?

Most of us want happiness, peace, contentment. These are all possible once we learn to manage the pain and disappointment and storms of our day to day. Because those storms will never end. Our inner happiness comes when we learn to find peace within regardless of what is occurring outside of us or inside our mental and physical states.

Life won't stop being what life is after you kick a morphine habit, or an eating disorder, or an alcohol addiction or a gambling obsession. Those difficulties that plagued you in the past will recur with different faces and varying problems to solve. Your strength and success lie in developing positive and healthy tools and strategies for living and moving forward. Your own inner work and mindfulness about your situation, whatever that looks like for you, are what will guide you and help you navigate through the changes, difficulties, and the celebrations that lie ahead.

To the best of my knowledge, Mrs. Dubose did not adopt a mindfulness practice, but she died "beholden to nothing and nobody." There is such a lightness and freedom and empowerment in knowing that you are your own master. You are the one who is deciding what your day will look like, and what your morning after will feel like.

Be *your* version of Mrs. Dubose. Know that you can be strong and brave. Find your Truth and take back your power.

Reflection

Position yourself comfortably in your quiet space. If writing appeals to you, have pen and paper ready, or better yet, a journal.

Close your eyes, and simply focus on your breath. Be aware of breathing in, breathing out, breathing in, breathing out, breathing in, breathing out.

The following questions or statements may be an aid to direct your inner work:

What are you afraid to face? What would be the worst thing that could happen if you chose to face it?

How would it feel to be able to truly let go of your compulsive behaviour?

Sacred Path Card #19
Painted Face

The Painted Face speaks of self-expression. It tells you to use your creativity in order to express your feelings, your talents, or your desires. Expressing who and what you are at any given moment is healing as well as productive. As you change and grow you may feel the need to alter the way in which others perceive you. Changing your appearance, attitudes, and activities to match the new you may be called for at this time.

The keynote is that this card asks you to open up and allow others to see your Medicine. In that way, you are offering a gift to others who may have need of your talents. Don't deny how you feel, what you think, or what you can offer the world. In truth and with grace it is now time to allow the Medicine of the Self to emerge. You will never lose face by presenting the true Self minus the self-importance. (Sams 163 – 164)

twenty-six

Sometimes, the simple things are more fun and meaningful than all the banquets in the world.

— E.A. Bucchianeri, *Brushstrokes of a Gadfly*

Learning to Have Fun

"I'm just going to have a couple of drinks because I want to be able to enjoy myself."

Famous last words. But also, a very common (mis)perception.

If you have spent most of your adult life with alcohol as an integral component of any social activity, any leisure pastime, any recreation or entertainment or any interaction at all, it seems so very bleak and impossible to imagine that anything can be fun or enjoyable without it. Intoxicants of all kinds are often a part of social functions, and many, if not most of us rely on them to overcome our anxieties and self-consciousness in social settings.

In my twenties, my alcohol abuse led to a pretty promiscuous lifestyle. Alcohol made me feel pretty and confident and flirtatious which often led to seductive dancing with an attractive male I'd just met in whatever bar I was at and ended with me waking up to the appalling reality and shameful remorse of yet another one-night stand in some seedy hotel room or stranger's apartment. Yeah. . .that sure was 'fun.'

Alcohol is so deceptive and causes such recklessness—I am so very grateful that I survived those incidents and did not end up with someone mentally unstable who could have inflicted serious physical harm. The emotional devastation was more than enough to work through. It has taken many years to have compassionate forgiveness towards myself for those behaviours and to let go of yet another reason for believing I'm a 'bad person.'

I always thought I was an extrovert, until I stopped drinking. It took a few years after that to realize I truly was more of an introvert. Given that I had a very social profession as a high school teacher, and was quite animated on the job, it came as a bit of a surprise that I actually preferred time alone or with close loved ones rather than a party scene. Very often the substance abuser loves a party because it's a legitimate excuse to partake, or more likely, over-indulge, as I most often did.

Choosing to let go of the compulsive behaviours does not mean that you will never have fun, will never be able to 'let loose' or will never enjoy a party. You will, however, need a different approach. And be prepared that initially it may be awkward and somewhat difficult, but this too shall pass. Yes, change is always difficult and painful, but there are treasures that await on the other side of all personal growth.

In my drinking days, I could at times be the life of the party, but more often than not I was definitely closing it down. More is better, right? It's only 1:00 or 2:00 am—there's still more booze, let's keep this thing going! Yeah. . .

When I was no longer drinking and then especially when I was no longer smoking or using any substance, I learned that I was good for about two to three hours of any party scene. After that, depending on what was being consumed, the conversations would start to deteriorate or become repetitive and inane, or ramp up if there was lots of alcohol imbibing. And given my introverted nature, after two to three hours I'm usually satiated socially anyway and am ready to recharge on my own.

I learned it's a good idea for me to plan my social engagements ahead of time. Giving myself an 'escape route' is a good idea; I find it helps me to enjoy the evening more, and often I'll stay later than I thought I might, but I know I don't *have* to. As much as possible I try to avoid feeling trapped in social situations that may be too uncomfortable or too tempting. If I feel there's a chance my resolve may be easily swayed, I prepare for that also.

I've learned to bring my own favorite non-alcoholic beverages and drink out of any fancy glass I choose. If I want my non-alcoholic beer in a wine glass, so be it. And I always thoroughly enjoy the food and allow myself to indulge as I'm not taking in the extra sugar in alcohol.

These are my choices, and yours may be different, but indulge yourself in any way that is safe and circumvents you feeling completely deprived.

The other beautiful bonus within all of this is that you will be in control of your faculties throughout the event, and will most likely wake the next morning without that horrendous dread, shame and remorse in the pit of your stomach due to regrets of the night's uncontrolled actions and conversations.

I relish the feeling of being fully aware, clear and present within interactions at all times. Previously it was more common for me to either withdraw in conversations due to my muddled state of mind or blunder through them incoherently and make an ass of myself. I much prefer the grace and dignity of being straight and clear and well spoken.

And I LOVE the morning after.

You may also find that once you stop relying on substances, intoxicant-filled social gatherings may no longer be that appealing. That's okay too. You'll be surprised to discover there are so many other ways to have fun. Maybe there are activities and hobbies you've always wanted to try but 'couldn't find the time' or maybe you didn't have the resources because all your money was being sucked away by your habits. There is a world of fun awaiting you.

Maybe you'll want to spend more time out in nature—hiking, camping, kayaking. Maybe you'll choose to explore different cooking styles or recipes. Maybe you'll have more money to spend on live entertainment or travel.

Be aware that your circle of friends and acquaintances may start changing. You may discover that you have less in common than you thought. And once the clouds and fog start clearing within your perception, this may become more and more apparent. This can be a very difficult transition time, and you may be surprised at the lack of authenticity in some of your friendships. It's pretty common for people to experience the 'Mexican crab' story from the previous chapter, and have to navigate through the difficult conversations with friends who may fear losing their drinking buddy or their partner in crime, or more truthfully, may fear having to look at their own detrimental behaviours. Rather than face that discomfort, they may unload their fears into all kinds of reasons why *you* shouldn't or don't want to make the change, and may feed your own fears about your new choices.

When we are not in our own best states, being true and authentic within ourselves, we can be quite manipulative in making sure that those close to us don't reach their better potentials either. I don't think it's with mal intent; sometimes we just don't want to lose our party buddy or our smoking buddy or our shop-a-holic buddy. And we listen to our friends tell us, "Aw, don't worry about it—you're fine! Everybody needs a release sometimes. It's nothing. You'll be fine. C'mon, let's go have some fun," etc.

People who genuinely care for you will support you and want the best for you.

And if you're starting to pursue some of those other dreams you've previously been putting on the back burner, you'll discover other friends, people of like mind with whom you resonate in a clearer way.

It can be a difficult path to find those new ways to enjoy yourself, but the purer joy and genuine pleasures that await are well worth the walk.

Reflection

Position yourself comfortably in your quiet space. If writing appeals to you, have pen and paper ready, or better yet, a journal.

Close your eyes, and simply focus on your breath. Be aware of breathing in, breathing out, breathing in, breathing out, breathing in, breathing out.

The following questions or statements may be an aid to direct your inner work:

In what ways are you no longer finding fun and enjoyment in activities that used to bring you pleasure?

Think of all the things that bring you joy that do not include any type of substance abuse.

Who are the people with whom you would enjoy sharing these types of activities?

What are the activities you can do on your own that bring you joy?

twenty-seven

The best way to find yourself is to lose yourself in the service of others.

– Mahatma Gandhi

Remember that the happiest people are not those getting more, but those giving more.

– H. Jackson Brown Jr.

It is in Giving

It is in giving that we receive.

It is in giving that we receive.

It is in giving that we receive.

I could continue stating this infinitely and still many would not hear it.

But why? Our society and culture and the media are constantly filling our ears and eyes with the getting, the acquiring, the achieving, the having, and the needing. And most of it is about 'stuff.' And because many of us have an innate desire to grow and become more than we already are, we confuse it with acquiring stuff and comparing ourselves to others and being lured and tempted with the messages of needing more and more and more.

Yes, we need shelter and food and clothing. We are more comfortable if we have homes and furniture and warm apparel, and we do love to decorate and upgrade—both our dwellings and ourselves. I have also been taken up with these pastimes and aspirations; when we are young and nesting and creating homes for ourselves and our families, who doesn't want to have nice things and be comfortable?

It's when all of this becomes our major focus and the impetus of our day that we lose sight of what is really important and what will bring us true happiness and fulfillment. We are all familiar with the unending craving for stuff; you buy that object you've been longing for, and within days or moments of having it, you desire something else. The want is never satiated.

But, why isn't it satiated? Why aren't we ever satisfied with the receiving of more?

What if: "We are put on this earth to serve."

This comment was made one evening in my wise women's group and I was struck by the simplicity and validity of the statement. I hadn't considered it before even though I was becoming more and more aware of the benefits and inner fulfillment I was experiencing the more that I gave to others.

The giving was not necessarily in objects or money or stuff; at times it was, but more so I had begun giving my time and energy and a listening ear and an offer of help, being consciously open to opportunities when I could be of some assistance to others, and acting on it whenever possible. It did sometimes include a gift of money, a donation, or a concrete, practical object of necessity. Most often I have given, and continue to give, of my time, and this I have found invaluable.

It is in Giving

As a parent, there has been nothing more fulfilling (or challenging) than being there for my children 24/7 as they were growing up, and then navigating through all their changing needs and expectations as they matured. It is here that I have truly experienced the gifts in giving, because it is impossible to articulate all that being their mother has given to me.

In my career as a high school teacher, I learned very early that the way to be most effective with my students was also to be open to their needs, and perhaps more importantly, to build connections with them. An educator can be a fount of knowledge and an expert in their field, but if that person has zero connection with the audience, all that important info can fall on deaf ears.

Connection is crucial to our human existence. We all want to be loved, and to have friends and to be with others who understand us, with whom we can resonate and help alleviate our isolation and inner and outer struggles and suffering. How can we give to another if we don't have any connection or understanding as to what they are needing from us?

There is an episode of Oprah Winfrey's *Super Soul Sunday* podcast where she interviews Thich Nhat Hanh, a renowned Vietnamese Buddhist monk and peace activist. I was struck when he spoke about 'deep listening.' He described it as listening intently with compassion when someone is suffering, rather than thinking about the advice you could give or your own opinion on the matter. Simply LISTEN. He believes that suffering can be somewhat released or diminished simply within the act of listening and sharing. Giving someone an opportunity to pour out their struggles to a compassionate friend who actually *hears* them can be healing in itself and does not need to include your counsel; that can come at a later time if it is requested.

The greatest gift you can offer another is a gift of connection: listening, encouraging, supporting, understanding, caring. The greatest gift we can give is our TIME. It takes time to show someone you care, and it takes awareness to know when your time could be needed and appreciated.

Unfortunately time is most often what we feel we *don't* have. Our society pushes us to be productive and to make enough money to have and acquire so much more than is actually needed for survival. And most of these desires are distractions from the things that will truly fulfill us, like relationships, and true connections with others, and time to listen to yourself and be aware of your own needs.

As I have become aware of the needs around me, and as I have responded with my time whenever possible, I have been amazed at the way my own needs have been taken care of and at the opportunities for fulfillment that have come my way. What I am suggesting is that you become more open and aware of those moments when a kind word, or a half hour chat, or a phone call might help someone in need.

There is an incredible joy and peace to be found with giving. If you open to those moments when you can be of service to others, and you act on them with a clear volition and with an intent of loving kindness, I can assure you that your own life will become richer on so many levels.

What you put out will come back to you. Not always in the next moment, but eventually, rest assured that you will be the recipient of the results of your actions and your thoughts.

The more you give, the more you will receive and the happier and more peaceful you will become. Trust that you will get what you need, do what is necessary to achieve that, and stay open to the ways you can serve those around you, those within the circle of your influence.

We all yearn to know the 'meaning of life.' I think it is possible to find meaning within your circle, and if you can give of yourself within that community of those you touch, you will reap the benefits within your own experience.

It truly is in giving that we receive.

Reflection

Position yourself comfortably in your quiet space. If writing appeals to you, have pen and paper ready, or better yet, a journal.

Close your eyes, and simply focus on your breath. Be aware of breathing in, breathing out, breathing in, breathing out, breathing in, breathing out.

The following questions or statements may be an aid to direct your inner work:

How does your compulsive/addictive behaviour detract from your openness and ability to give of yourself or spend quality time with others?

Think back to ways you have given of yourself in the past; how did this make you feel?

What are some ways that you can reach out to others at this time?

twenty-eight

Change is the law of life, and those who look only to the past and present are certain to miss the future.

— John F. Kennedy

The secret of change is to focus all of your energy not on fighting the old, but on building the new.

— Dan Millman, *Way of the Peaceful Warrior*

2020

Crazy times, yet not so crazy.

Unbelievable change, yet not so unbelievable.

On many levels, it's brilliant.

We are being forced to STOP, to slow down, to recognize what is essential, to reduce consumptions, to spend time with family. . .with our very lives as collateral. Pretty high stakes. Pretty strong message.

And this perspective is easy for me, at this point, as I am healthy, and my family and friends are healthy. COVID-19 has not had drastic repercussions in my life—at this point.

I live in Canada where we have a wonderful health care system that takes care of everyone. Our government has been incredibly helpful in giving financial aid to those in need at this time. I am fortunate to be retired, and with a pension, so my financial situation has not really been affected.

And yet all over the world there are others whose lives have been tragically altered, and in some cases, lost. The impact of this virus has as many different faces as there are humans on the planet. Each one of us is experiencing a unique response and individual repercussions.

My heart goes out to those who are struggling financially, or with their health or the health of a loved one. My heart is also with those working in areas of the medical system on the frontlines, being overloaded with COVID-19 cases, having to care for them as they die without the comfort of their loved ones present, and being fearful, as a caregiver, of the very real possibility of being inflicted with the virus yourself. I can't imagine the fear and stress of any of these situations.

This pandemic has such extreme and varied repercussions on us all, worldwide. What an incredible example to bring us to our knees, to surrender to the reality that we are not invincible, not in control, not the masters of the planet. Not by a long shot.

Not unlike Life itself.

In many ways, COVID-19 has simply magnified reality.

With all the distractions bombarding us, it's been very easy to lose sight of what really *was* and what really *is*.

COVID-19 has crashed through our distorted perspectives and is shining a glaring spotlight on our previous 'normal.' What is the virus showing us? Absolute uncertainty; that nothing is in our control.

It never has been. But we feel more comfortable in deluding ourselves that it is.

It is showing us that death is ever imminent. Yup—it is where we are ALL headed, without question, and without knowing when or how.

It is showing us what is essential to survival. And it's not a haircut, or an exotic vacation, or a new outfit, or a congregation of many people being physically together for whatever purpose.

It is showing us that change is constant, moment by moment, and nothing is permanent, especially not our prior lifestyle and treatment of this planet, our source of life.

It is showing us that WE ARE ALL IN THIS TOGETHER. We are all part of the same thing, and in giving this virus to another—in hurting another—we are actually harming ourselves, our own survival.

It is showing us the invaluable importance of our BREATH. Yes, we know we need to breathe in order to survive, but it's so obvious that it's crucial on so many levels; so many mindfulness and meditation techniques begin with the breath, the one thing we cannot survive without.

It is showing us the importance of managing and being mindful of our emotions and reactions. They can really be amped up at this time, without a doubt. Knowing that each extreme feeling *will* pass, *will* change, *will* ease, and is manageable, can greatly help in easing our anxiety right now.

It is giving many of us much needed time for reflection, and inner processing. For some it is almost an 'enforced' retreat.

It is giving us time to reach out to others, with more than just a text. Even though we cannot physically be together, thanks to technology right now there are so many ways to connect and share.

It is giving us an opportunity to change, before it may be too late; before we do more irreparable damage to our planet, our life source.

And because most of us resist change at all costs, we need to have our most precious possession as collateral—our LIVES.

Yup, this is serious, folks.

This is not a 'maybe' situation.

Our choice. My choice. Your choice.

On a personal note, I am so grateful to be fully present in this moment, rather than choosing to be in the la-la land of substance abuse through it all. It doesn't make it any more or less scary or unnerving, but it does feel good to be relatively calm, taking it in stride, and feeling (mostly) optimistic about possible futures. Knowing each morning when I wake that yes, this is where the world is right now, and yet I am feeling pretty strong within myself: I am well, I am present to each moment as it unfolds.

Not surprisingly, this isn't the case for many of us. I keep seeing articles about the increase in alcohol consumption and binging on a variety of levels. It's one of the most difficult time periods the majority of us have ever experienced, so no wonder. But many of us will need to face those dragons of substance abuse at some point in our futures.

I have no idea how long this will last; none of us do. It's a glaring example of the uncertainty that truly is always present. We just can't deny it anymore.

I'm so very grateful for my meditation practice and the tools I've gained and the strides I've made which are all serving me well at this time. This stuff works. As my wise brother has said, "No steps on a spiritual path are ever lost, no matter how small." And that is true no matter what personal growth journey we are choosing.

Keep taking your steps, now more than ever. Grow your tools, see the gifts of growth that are presented within difficulty and adversity, and rise to their offering.

Reflection

Position yourself comfortably in your quiet space. If writing appeals to you, have pen and paper ready, or better yet, a journal.

Close your eyes, and simply focus on your breath. Be aware of breathing in, breathing out, breathing in, breathing out, breathing in, breathing out.

The following questions or statements may be an aid to direct your inner work:

How do you normally respond when great change is thrust upon you?

Think back to a time when you resisted change. What were the results and repercussions of your actions?

Think of a time when you accepted great change and were able to roll with it. What were the results and repercussions of your actions?

twenty-nine

I'm not telling you it's going to be easy - I'm telling you it's going to be worth it.

— Art Williams

A Taste of Freedom

I am presently six months into a period of abstinence. Nothing earth-shattering about that—I've been here before.

But maybe I haven't. This feels quite different.

This isn't a time of endurance and counting the days to say I made it a year, with the ever-lurking comfort that I can take it up again if I choose.

This is different. There has been a definite shift.

I'm not experiencing that craving to distract and distort my reality, to numb my pain or escape my feelings. And I can truly say there's been no end of 'tests.'

It's April 2020 and we are presently into our second month of isolation and social distancing in the global outbreak of the COVID-19 pandemic.

Now, *there's* a little cause for escape, I'd say! It's like the ultimate time to veg out and enter la-la land and distract yourself from a really unnerving and uncomfortable reality, stuck in your home, nowhere to go, not much to do, and zero responsibility other than to STAY HOME. There's never been a better or more perfect time to stay high!

And I have no desire.

Plus, for personal family reasons I am spending much of this time presently with my daughter at our family cottage—complete isolation—and it's THE COTTAGE.

My ultimate trigger.

And I have no desire. No craving. No discomfort.

I'm still 'godsmacked' about it all. Have I really turned a corner and made a shift that's been five decades of struggle?

I shouldn't be so surprised, I guess, as truly there's nothing I've worked harder at overcoming. And I think a crucial component of this present success is my meditation practice, and learning to be present with what is, knowing it will not last, because nothing lasts. Trying to avoid our pain only compounds our suffering. Accepting it and acknowledging it allows it to pass through quickly and makes space for other moments to arise, and also pass.

When I feel those moments of unrest—boredom, frustration, sadness, anger, fear—I sit, if possible, even if it's only for a short time. I sit and know that it will pass.

And it's not that the pain and discomfort have become less; in fact, the more you practise, the more aware you are and the more your emotions feel intensified, both positive and negative. More intense, yet shorter-lived. More poignant, but less problematic. And gratefully there are far more frequent times of calm and relative contentment. It becomes easier to navigate through the storms and upsets of daily life, to diffuse the knee-jerk reactions of the past.

So for now I am basking in the celebration of success.

I've earned it, and it's been a long struggle, a long time of wanting to be on the other side of this. Daily—many times each day, in fact—I celebrate myself. It's a refreshing and well-deserved switch from the far-too-familiar self-abuse.

There's a lovely calm in waking every morning with a clear head and no remorse. To know that my feelings—whatever they are—are genuine and not compounded by distortion. . .other than my own thinking, of course. Still and always so much to learn.

I keep walking.

~

Fast forward and it's eight months later, and as a planet we're still in the midst of a pandemic and have been in various states of lockdown and isolation over the past year, with no end in sight at this point. I have had the opportunity to be living at the meditation centre for most of the past year, working in the office as a volunteer and residing in a lovely cozy cabin on the outskirts of the centre property, surrounded by the most amazing forest. Gratitude abounds.

While many people I know have found this time of reclusion beneficial—a time for slowing down, personal reflection, re-evaluation of values—many people, especially elders, are struggling in varying degrees, with the imposed isolation, with financial hardship, with health issues, etc. My heart goes out to them.

I feel so very fortunate to be able to spend this time here, working with a few others in maintaining the centre residences, community buildings and grounds, with the opportunity to meditate in the meditation hall every day, and I take none of it for granted.

I'm including this here because I feel the need to acknowledge that perhaps I've been able to manage my compulsive behaviours more easily due to my present living situation. Would I still be clear and intoxicant-free if I were living on my own and dealing with these challenging times? I don't know.

What I do know is, regardless of whether it's been easier for me being here, I've still been rewiring my behaviour patterns for the past year. Living here with only a handful of others and maintaining my practice has often been very demanding and there have been many occasions of self-evaluation and personal growth. I don't think it's an accident that I happen to be here at this time. And the more that I face inner struggles and find positive ways of working through them without succumbing to the escape of intoxicants, the more those relentless ruts are being filled in and the more I am rerouting my path in different and healthier directions.

I'm not kidding myself; I know the possibility of a relapse is always present. It's been too many decades of ups and downs to pretend otherwise. But in the acceptance of that fact is also empowerment, because it always comes down to *my choice*. And the longer that I continue to make better choices and move forward, the more I know that those triggers will pass, the more aware I am of my self-talk, the more quickly the temptation subsides.

The more I trust this taste of freedom.

I struggle at times with the right phrase to express where I'm at—"straight" doesn't have the same meaning as it had when I was younger; "sober" implies alcohol abstinence in my mind; "in recovery" has too many shades of AA to it for me (with the ultimate in respect to AA and all that it offers to so many).

I like to think I'm "intoxicant-free." That covers it without implying other references, plus I love relishing in the idea of feeling free. So much of our true happiness can be found in letting go, releasing our attachments to things—and people—that may not be how we want them to be, or may not last, because nothing lasts forever. True happiness can be found in letting go of the craving and grasping and dissatisfaction when we think we are so sure of what we need or desire or can't be happy without. Letting go is the ultimate freedom, and letting go, bit by bit, of my desire to escape or distract or numb, and allowing myself to be present in what is in my reality, is truly giving me a taste of freedom and moments of joy and real happiness.

This stuff works.

Reflection

Position yourself comfortably in your quiet space. If writing appeals to you, have pen and paper ready, or better yet, a journal.

Close your eyes, and simply focus on your breath. Be aware of breathing in, breathing out, breathing in, breathing out, breathing in, breathing out.

The following questions or statements may be an aid to direct your inner work:

If you could celebrate yourself, how would you do it? What would you say to yourself?

What does freedom look like to you?

thirty

Bottom line is, even if you see 'em coming, you're not ready for the big moments. No one asks for their life to change, not really. But it does. So what are we, helpless? Puppets? No. The big moments are gonna come. You can't help that. It's what you do afterwards that counts. That's when you find out who you are.

— Joss Whedon

Defining Moments

There are those 'still photograph' moments in our memories, those life-shifting a-ha moments and godsmacks which shape our character and often change our course irrevocably.

Some are obviously fortuitous and gratifying. Some are frightening and painful and we may not see the gifts within their strike until later, or maybe never. But either way, there is a driving force within these that defines our future.

Until my mid-twenties I was incredibly trusting and naïve to some of the ways of the world and the motives of some of our species. That changed abruptly when I was the victim of the rape at age twenty-four; anyone who has suffered through this knows too well that it never really leaves you. And then within that same year, I became involved with that man who was a complete con, a fake, someone who preyed on trusting women in order to take their money, break their hearts, and steal their trust.

It was not a good year. A couple good knocks like that can certainly adjust your perspective. It took a long while—and a lot of wine—to climb out of that well.

There are important moments that occurred during the next ten years, but one of my most favourite stills is looking down on my first born, the moment I fully realized that it was true, it had really happened—this was my baby girl, and I was a mother.

My pregnancy had been overdue by two weeks, and I was riddled with anxiety that something would go wrong, that every pregnant woman 'gets the prize' of a healthy baby except me.

I loved my oldest brother's encouragement at this time: "How can you be upset? You're a miracle waiting to happen!" How beautiful is that?

Due to complications, she was delivered by C-section after about thirty-six hours of labour, and shortly after she was born I collapsed into an exhausted sleep. A few hours later the nurse woke me to breastfeed, and one of my most beautiful memories is that moment of just the two of us, gazing at her precious perfection—this was my baby girl. She had made my dream come true, and she gave me my first taste of the profundity of unconditional love. Of course, NOTHING was the same after that, in all wondrous and magical and challenging ways.

There are many moments in between, and this one has already been mentioned, but that horrific moment of waking up from an alcoholic blackout and seeing a hole burnt in the table from an abandoned lit cigarette, with my two young girls sleeping down the hall, was a godsmack for which I am eternally grateful. That I managed to turn that corner without causing physical harm to my children is a gift and a blessing.

It was a couple years later, when our girls were still very young, that we started our Temagami summers. Temagami is a town situated on a glorious lake of the same name, and the surrounding area is the quintessential landscape and experience of the unbridled beauty that is northern Ontario: pristine fresh-water lakes and lush forests as far as the eye can see and the canoe can be paddled. We spent nine magical summers camping on Crown land on a small lake in the middle of nowhere, staying anywhere from three to six weeks, with no technology or screens and one cell phone for emergencies. I have always loved camping and living outdoors, and this was the ultimate. We were fifteen kilometres from the town which had less than 1,000 population, though it did boast the best chip stand and chicken wings on the planet, in our humble (and well-tested) opinion.

There were millions of moments, but what is framed in my mind are the mornings: I would awaken before anyone else, unfold my camping 'recliner' seat and sit with my coffee and my journal and greet the sun's rising over the lake. To this day I consider it my 'Spirit Spot.' I had stopped drinking a couple of years prior to our summers there, so I am grateful that I did not bring that baggage to this special place. There were many difficult moments triggered in our marital struggles, given that our family of four was on our own here for the most part, but there were also so many wonderful memories of happy family times, feeling one with nature and being fully present with my children.

Fast forward through their childhood to the teen years, with countless hours of marriage counselling over a twelve-year period. We are in Australia as a family while I am on a teaching exchange. It is an unforgettable year of magical and challenging experiences, which also included the moment I knew my marriage was over.

Our daughters had trained for six months to join in an incredible endeavour called the Kokoda Challenge. Each year, there are two hikes that run simultaneously in the Gold Coast Hinterland; one is fifty kilometres and one is ninety-six kilometres—nonstop. The hikes are to commemorate a heroic feat of courage, endurance, sacrifice and mateship by Australian soldiers during World War II in Papua New Guinea, when they were attacked by the Japanese. It is also a fundraising event for youth in Australia, and an endurance and character-shaping experience like nothing I have ever witnessed. I could go on for hours about the honour of supporting both our girls as they trained for and completed these challenges, and I have never been so overwhelmed with pride, love, humility and wonder at their achievements.

And within this memorable weekend of life-shifting memories, there was also the straw that broke my marriage's back. I'll not share details as, though I'm willing to be transparent about my own life and transgressions, I will not share those of others. Suffice it to say that anyone who has gone through the ending of a long and difficult relationship will understand that there is a moment when you know. When every stone has been overturned, every attempt has been made, every second, third, hundredth chance has been given, and the account just bottomed out. You're done. There's nothing left.

I say my sixtieth year is tattooed on my soul; homage to that year and that particular weekend is literally tattooed on my wrist.

Moving on through the next seven years, and the suffering of separation and finding my way as a single (but happier) woman again, and the pain and struggle in the ending of a thirty-year friendship with one of my closest friends, and then, the icing on my cake of lifelong spiritual searching—taking my first ten-day retreat at the Ontario Vipassana Centre. Definitely one of the fortuitous stills; I remember completing the course in a daze of wonder at the brilliance of what was being offered. And people told me I glowed when I came home. I know I was glowing and vibrating within. That experience has definitely changed the trajectory of my years since then.

There are many, many more, some that have already been shared on previous pages; it's not necessary to list them all here and now.

But I am choosing to write about *these* monumental defining moments.

Because what I've realized is that most of my defining moments have nothing to do with alcohol or substance abuse.

And that in itself is another defining moment! Most of the events and situations that I see as having the most profound influence in shaping me as a person did not include alcohol or drugs. So, if I'm seeing myself as a person whose overriding self-concept is as an alcoholic or compulsive drug user, maybe it's not true. At least, maybe it's not the biggest truth. Maybe it's just a belief I've been feeding myself for years.

Maybe what's most important about who I am are those other 'carving' moments. I again borrow words from the wonderful Elizabeth Gilbert, who spoke during an interview about the tsunami of grief she often experiences in the loss of Rayya Elias, the love of her life, as a moment that "comes when it wants to, and it *carves* you out." (Popova)

We all have them, we all know them—those moments that become part of you because they've been carved into your being. And it doesn't matter if the sculpting has been happy or horrific, the end result is that you are changed, you are different, you have moved into something else.

Those are the moments that define you, that create your definition. And more important than the actual moments are your choices and decisions that result from those moments.

We are the creators of our definition.

Reflection

Position yourself comfortably in your quiet space. If writing appeals to you, have pen and paper ready, or better yet, a journal.

Close your eyes, and simply focus on your breath. Be aware of breathing in, breathing out, breathing in, breathing out, breathing in, breathing out.

The following questions or statements may be an aid to direct your inner work:

List your defining moments. How many of them are consequences of your compulsive behaviour?

What changes did they cause within?

Does your list of defining moments support your beliefs about yourself, or contradict them?

Creator Said

Creator said: "I want to hide something from the humans until they are ready for it. It is the realization that they create their own reality."

The eagle said, "Give it to me. I will take it to the moon."

The Creator said, "No. One day they will go there and find it."

The salmon said, "I will bury it on the bottom of the ocean."

The Creator said, "No. They will go there, too."

The buffalo said, "I will bury it on the Great Plains."

The Creator said, "They will cut into the skin of the earth and find it even there."

Grandmother, who lives in the breast of Mother Earth, and who has no physical eyes but sees with spiritual eyes, said, "Put it inside of them."

And the Creator said, "It is done."

Hopi Creation Story (Spirit Quest Programs)

Epilogue

Life is a gift and a challenge in its myriad of possibilities, consequences, rewards, obstacles, joys, difficulties, and of course, beauty and magic.

My personal journey continues. It will never end as long as I continue breathing.

My inner shift is feeling more and more trustworthy, and the triggers cause less and less reaction. It continues to amaze me. It works. It is possible.

A few of my early reviewers asked me if I was comfortable in sharing so much of my personal experience. Hell no. It's like cutting yourself open to the depths of your soul for all to see.

But I think it's key to continuing my growth and more importantly, it can help you in yours. The most crucial piece in my process has been knowing I am not alone, not unique, not the only one who has experienced situations and behaviours I'm not proud of; knowing that others whom I admire overcame worse realities in their own pasts and grew to reclaim not only their lives, but their grace and dignity.

I can share my past because it no longer is. I no longer live there. And transparency is empowering and can make you unbreakable.

I share these experiences because they are my 'credentials.' I don't pretend to be a therapist, I don't have a list of academic accomplishments after my name and I don't profess that my way is THE way. But this is what I have lived and the path I have walked.

Sharing my pain and my shame and my guilt gives permission to others to do the same, even if it means only opening up to it within themselves. We cannot begin to heal until we can look at the dis-ease and dis-order that is wreaking havoc in our lives. In order to let them go, we have to acknowledge their existence.

If you are not yet able to love yourself enough to change, think of someone or something else that deserves a better and more fuller you. Start for them.

My children gave me my reason, and for that, and on so many other levels, I am so very grateful to them. As my editor Hannah said, "Your story is in part a love story for your children."

True that.

My daughters are my teachers. The Universe uses what you love and cherish the most to show you your way.

And this is also a love story for myself. If we cannot love ourselves, we cannot fully and openly love others.

In order to save or help others, we must save and help ourselves.

We can't shield ourselves or others from pain; it is inevitable. If we try to shield others from pain, we are robbing them of their inherent possibilities of growth and becoming.

What we can do is learn from our pain and discomfort to become our best and fullest selves.

If you love someone, show them your resilience, your ability to learn and adapt, your openness to truth, so that they may also learn and grow.

So, although this was not a conscious intention as I was writing, this is, in part, a love story for my children, for myself—and for you.

Reclaim your grace. Remember who you are.

You are your own creation.

Resources

If you are interested in finding out more about mindfulness and meditation, please check out the following websites:

Shinzen Young

Besides residential retreats in both the United States and Canada, Shinzen offers many virtual opportunities, including his Home Practice Program and Life Practice Program:

www.shinzen.org/

Unified Mindfulness

Also a part of Shinzen's organization is the Unified Mindfulness program with learning and teaching opportunities offered:

unifiedmindfulness.com/

Vipassana Meditation

Vipassana meditation as taught by S.N. Goenka in the tradition of Sayagyi U Ba Khin is offered worldwide. Find the centre nearest you:

www.dhamma.org/en-US/index

Acknowledgements

Most of our accomplishments are manifested not only through our efforts but with the support and encouragement of others. In this case, there is a need to acknowledge the support in creating this book, but most importantly I recognize those wonderful beings who have encouraged me in and contributed to my personal growth.

Many thanks to Friesen Press and Gillian Hebert for a smooth and well-supported publishing process, and to Nancy Leach, a fellow meditator and author, for her recommendations and support during this process. Hannah Gardiner, what a serendipitous turn of events that led to your discerning editing and insightful organization of the writing. I'm so very grateful for your contributions. Nancy Friday, Crysta Fernandez, Diane Frederick, Elaine Jacob, Rose Skrapits and Rick Walker—thank you for taking the time to review my writing and giving me such valuable feedback and encouragement. I'm also very grateful to my daughter Kody for her meticulous proofreading, and to my daughter Willow for her artistic flair in bringing 'the dragon' to life.

To my brother John, with whom I share far more similarities than is sometimes comfortable, I am so grateful for our relationship and the heartfelt support that is always there. Bob Wagester, thanks for your friendship and guidance in my spiritual journey. You always say the right thing whether I want to hear it or not. Maliha Safrani, in your wisdom and direction you have been such an inspiring role model for me, and I am so very grateful for our time together. Jassy Narayan, your wisdom, grace and insight to say exactly what

I needed to hear in so many situations have been invaluable in my journey. Robert Rombough, thanks for helping me to know that I am not a bad person, and for your invaluable support and presence throughout my life. Rick Walker, my walking memory—you remember every detail about my past and have continued to love me anyway. It's wonderful sharing so many similar perspectives on our journey through this life. Paula Anstett, thanks for so many meaningful and inspirational conversations, shared perspectives, wonderful memories and personal growth opportunities over the years. And thanks to Wanda Goodwin, Donna and Harry Vanderzand, and Cheryl Hambly, for the support and lifelong friendships as we forge our way on this journey.

To my mom, Diane, I'm so grateful for these last few years of truly appreciating one another, and that goes also for my other brothers, Ed and Richard—we are very fortunate in the relationships we share. Thanks to my dad, the late John Krynicki, for the many gifts and strengths he passed on to us. To Jerry, our years together provided so many opportunities for growth and change. Thank you for co-parenting our beautiful daughters. And to Toby, Amber, Drew, Justin, Delijah and Daija—thanks for giving me more opportunities to love and learn and expand my family circle.

And, of course, so much love and gratitude to Kody and Willow. To Kody, my beautiful inside-and-out firstborn, thank you for constantly showing me new ways to grow and for being a role model in your caring and consideration of others. And to Willow, my radiant and insightful old soul daughter, I am forever grateful for your direct and pure wisdom that stops me in my tracks when I need redirection. You have both enriched my life beyond words. . . though perhaps it's been expressed in these last 48,000.

Works Cited

Cain, Susan. *Quiet.* New York: Crown Publishers, 2012.

"Creator Said." *Spirit Quest Programs, Facebook.* 24 November 2018. www.facebook.com/spiritquestprograms/posts/creator-said-i-want-to-hide-something-from-the-humans-until-they-are-ready-for-i/5092228262567291/. Accessed 12 November 2020.

"F. Scott Fitzgerald." *The Baltimore Literary Heritage Project.* baltimoreauthors.ubalt.edu/writers/fscottfitzgerald.htm#:~:text=A%20heavy%20drinker%20throughout%20his,working%20on%20The%20Last%20Tycoon. Accessed 2 March 2021.

Gilbert, Elizabeth [@elizabeth_gilbert_writer]. "I wanted to be Florence Nightingale." *Instagram*, 10 June, 2019, www.elizabethgilbert.com/onward/.

Gilbert, Elizabeth [@elizabeth_gilbert_writer]. "Be who you needed when you were younger."@ShareTheseWords, 11 November 2019, www.elizabethgilbert.com/onward/.

Goldstein, Joseph & Kornfield, Jack. *Seeking the Heart of Wisdom.* Boston: Shambhala, 1987.

"How Shame Feeds Addiction." *Verta Health (formerly Addiction Campuses).* 15 March 2019. How Shame Feeds Addiction (vertavahealth.com). Accessed 7 January 2021.

Kuja, Marie-Claire. "The Story of the Crabs in the Bucket." 11 February 2016.www.worldpulse.com/community/users/kujamac12/posts/64304. Accessed 16 May 2020.

Lee, Harper. *To Kill a Mockingbird.* New York: J. P. Lippincott & Co., 1960.

Neff, Kristin. *Self-compassion: stop beating yourself up and leave insecurity behind.* New York: HarperCollins, 2011.

Popova, Maria. *Brain Pickings.* "Elizabeth Gilbert on Love, Loss and How to Move Through Grief as Grief Moves Through You." www.brainpickings.org/2018/10/17/elizabeth-gilbert-ted-podcast-love-loss/. Accessed 5 June 2020.

Porter, Eleanor H. *Pollyanna – The Glad Book.* New York: Grosset & Dunlap, 1938.

Sams, Jamie. *Sacred Path Cards – The discovery of self through native teachings.* New York: HarperCollins, 1990.

Schwartz, Allan N. "Of Self-hatred and Self-Compassion." *MentalHelp.net.* 20 March 2019. Of Self-Hatred and Self-Compassion - Depression Resources, Education About Depression and Unipolar Depression (mentalhelp.net). Accessed 7 January 2021.

"Two Wolves – A Cherokee Legend." *First People of American and Canada – Turtle Island.* www.firstpeople.us/FP-Html-Legends/TwoWolves-Cherokee.html. Accessed 2 February 2021.

Young, Shinzen. *The Science of Enlightenment: How meditation works.* Boulder, CO: Sounds True, 2016.

Printed in Canada